Lent & Easter
Readings
from IONA

D1037732

*To Marty + Linda –
friends + fellow travellers,
much love,
Alison xx*

Lent & Easter Readings from IONA

Neil Paynter (ed)

WILD GOOSE PUBLICATIONS

Readings © the individual contributors
Compilation © 2001 Neil Paynter
First published 2002 by
Wild Goose Publications, Fourth Floor, Savoy House,
140 Sauchiehall Street, Glasgow G2 3DH,
the publishing division of the Iona Community. Scottish Charity No. SCO03794.
Limited Company Reg. No. SCO96243.

ISBN 1 901557 62 6

Cover design © 2001 Wild Goose Publications

The publishers gratefully acknowledge the support of the Drummond Trust,
3 Pitt Terrace, Stirling FK8 2EY in producing this book.

A catalogue record for this book is available from the British Library.

Distributed in Australia by Willow Connection Pty Ltd, Unit 4A, 3-9 Kenneth Road, Manly Vale, NSW 2093, Australia, and in New Zealand by Pleroma Christian Supplies, Higginson St., Otane 4170, Central Hawkes Bay, New Zealand.

Permission to reproduce any part of this work in Australia
or New Zealand should be sought from Willow Connection.

Printed by Bell & Bain, Thornliebank, Glasgow

Contents

To companions on Iona
1997–2001
With love and thanks

Introduction

George MacLeod, the Founder of the Iona Community, once wrote:

The Bible is the most profound dramatisation of you ... The historic story of Christ, the outside story of Christ, suddenly emerges as the inner story of yourself – and it's this inner story, this inner parallel, that really makes the Bible inspired, so that to your condition it becomes the living Word of God.[1]

There is always the temptation to read these words and, indeed, to read the Bible, as being about the dramatisation of *me*, and Christ's story as the inner story of *myself*. And it is precisely because we can discern in the scriptures our own personal experiences of loss and love and betrayal, of suffering and hope, mediated to us through the experiences of other people in other times and places, that their stories, and above all the Christ story, have such power to comfort and encourage, to chasten and challenge and inspire us. We identify with the *dramatis personae*, we read ourselves into the text.

But if we restrict ourselves to this kind of individual reading, we run the risk of missing the point completely. Though we each have our moments of feeling that 'no one suffers quite like me', it is just then that we are actually more like everybody else than we care to admit. For the stories, and the story, are actually the dramatisation of *us*, the inner story of *ourselves*, humankind in all our diversity and similarity; and although the *via crucis*, the way of the cross, may take as many forms as the relentless parade of human misery we see on the nightly news, the experience of loss and love and betrayal, of suffering and hope, is universal.

It is in solidarity with this corporate experience that people enter into Lent, Holy Week and Easter observation. In prayer, reading, meditation and solitude, followers of Jesus may practise a measure of interior withdrawal and reflection, in which to look with some honesty at the wilderness places in our hearts and lives, to remember and name our own temptations and frailties and to hear again the call to conversion, to turning as the prodigal son did and heading for home. But we do so in the company of others. The great liturgical drama of Passiontide and Easter worship is a vivid reminder of the *us*. It locates us firmly in our humanity, inviting us to discover that it is only in the sharing of our human vulnerability and frailty that our potential for resurrection is to be found.

In his journal about a Lenten period in his monastery, the American contemplative and peacemaker Thomas Merton wrote:

Brother B. – a Mexican from Texas: what he thinks might be 'faults' are in reality the wounds that come from being poor. The poor man is, and remains vulnerable. How can the really poor, the really 'hurt' survive in a place like this? We are not so vulnerable, and we wound others, even when we are being 'good', perhaps especially then.[2]

It is a hard thing to admit the truth of this, to recognise the extent to which violence, injustice, oppression and cruelty are most powerful when their perpetrators are most convinced of their own righteousness, their own justification. We who are habitually scandalised by everyone except ourselves see this more clearly in others, less so in our own small justifications. The Easter experience is a journey towards recognising our complicity – but also to seeing the way beyond it.

O Christ our enlightener,
Once and for all,
you broke the link between suffering and punishment,
erased the line between deserving and undeserving
and invited the unseeing to open their eyes to the truth about themselves.
Doing this, you revealed yourself,
became vulnerable.
Preserve us from the defendedness that makes us vicious,
give us insight to see the structures of injustice by which we profit,
and grace to cherish all people in our vulnerability,
knowing that we all live within your love.[3]

This book of readings shares something of the Lent and Easter story of *us* – an us which is both Irish nationalist and Ulster Unionist, both American and Afghan, both Palestinian and Israeli, which is Moslem and Jewish and Christian and Buddhist and Hindu and atheist. In following Jesus on the way of the cross, we come face to face with the tragedy that *'Palestinians and Israelis have so much in common … their longing for that shalom or salaam which are only a syllable away from each other …' (Palm Sunday)* and yet that a vast, hostile distance of injustice, fear, racism, violence and death is contained within that single syllable. There are so many single syllables of distance, and yet so many people who are closer than breathing in their longing for love, hope, new life. What, or who, can span the distance? In a world bleeding with images of crucifixion, where is resurrection?

As the Easter readings in the book powerfully reiterate, perhaps one step is the recognition that Christ is also mocked in the little children jeered and threatened on their way to school, and Christ is also crucified in the Palestinian schoolgirl shot in her classroom, in the Israeli baby blown up by the car bomb, in the New York workers whose building was turned into a lethal weapon against them, and that Mary still weeps in the Afghan mother whose three children have just been killed, and in the wife waiting for the fire fighter who never came home. To recognise that is to recognise that it was our common humanity that went to the cross – and it is only in our common humanity that we can be raised.

The raising to new life of our humanness is most often expressed and affirmed in small things: in quiet, undemonstrative kindness, in tentative reaching-out across many kinds of barriers, in resistance against all kinds of dehumanisation and demonisation, in persistence against the odds, in continuing to create out of destruction, in the imagination of joy and wonder, and in triumphs, however small, of justice. These are also in this book, the testimonies of those who bear witness to the power of love against the love of power, and who keep alive the rumour that somewhere there is singing, somewhere people dance, and everywhere, even in the darkest places, love rises up unconquerable to meet us again.

Kathy Galloway

1   from *Daily Readings with George MacLeod*, ed. Ron Ferguson (Wild Goose Publications, 2001)

2   from *The Journals of Thomas Merton*, ed. Patrick Hart (Harper Collins, published in several volumes)

3   by Kathy Galloway from *Worship Resources for Unemployment Sunday 2002* (Church Action on Poverty)

Invocation for Lent

Into the dark world
a snowdrop comes,
a blessing of hope and peace
carrying within it a green heart:
symbol of God's renewing love.
Come to inhabit our darkness, Lord Christ,
for dark and light are alike to you.
May nature's white candles of hope
remind us of your birth
and lighten our journey
through Lent and beyond.

Kate McIlhagga

Ash Wednesday

*Dietrich Bonhoeffer talks about the need for 'holy worldly' people –
followers of Jesus who live in the world but who are sustained by an
arcane, or secret, discipline of prayer. 'Contemplation' or 'action' are
false alternatives. Both are involved in a Christian lifestyle. A person
who prays deeply will be driven to act against injustice. Similarly, a
Christian who is engaged in the problems of the world will be driven
to prayer. Contemplation need not be escapism, a turning one's back
on the world which God loves. Prayer is at the heart of a genuine
Christian radicalism – one which truly gets to the root of the matter.*

Ron Ferguson

Readings:
Joel 2:12–13, Isaiah 58:6–9

Ash Wednesday

Leader:	Choose this day whom you will serve;
ALL:	WE WILL CHOOSE THE LIVING GOD.
Leader:	The road is narrow that leads to life;
ALL:	WE WILL WALK THE WAY OF CHRIST.
Leader:	Faith is not our holding on
ALL:	FAITH IS LETTING GO.
Leader:	We offer more than words, O God;
ALL:	WE OFFER YOU OUR LIVES.

Reflection

Twice over recent years I have been fortunate enough to have been on Iona for Ash Wednesday. Usually it falls within the period of staff training just before the start of the season at the Iona Community's islands centres during which the members of the resident group, some just arrived, some continuing from the previous year, prepare themselves for the demanding task of welcoming and providing hospitality for the guests who come to Iona Abbey and the MacLeod Centre for the week-long programmes that run from just before Easter until October.

Over the winter months worship on Iona takes place in the Michael Chapel just behind the main Abbey buildings. As we gathered for the Ash Wednesday service this year the sun was streaming through the window behind the communion table, the reflected light off the Sound of Iona –

calm for once – intensifying the contrast between the bare white walls and the dark wood of the stalls where we sat silently. There was a strong sense of our togetherness and the significance and solemnity of the occasion.

The service proceeded – scripture, prayer, a quiet song, and the ritual of the ashes, on the palm of the hand for some, on the forehead for others. It is only relatively recently that I, as a Presbyterian, have come to experience and appreciate some of the rich dimensions of other traditions. And Lent has come to mean more and more over the years as a preparation for the demanding journey through Holy Week that culminates in the celebration of Easter.

Ash Wednesday of course marks the start of the period of Lenten fasting. It reminds us of the self-denial and self-discipline that is in fact integral to the way of the cross. It is not about self-abasement or self-advertisement: Matthew's account of the Sermon on the Mount contains Jesus's cautionary words about over-demonstrative fasting (Matthew 6:16–17); and the German theologian Dietrich Bonhoeffer encouraged a thoroughly discreet approach in this area. It might well be asked how ashes on the forehead measure up to his call for an 'arcane discipline'! Lent is rather a time for self-appraisal, for the kind of repentance that neither wallows in factitious self-loathing nor seeks escape in specious excuses. It requires a healthy realism about ourselves, so that we can face up to and accept responsibility for our mistakes and shortcomings, and realism about the nature and purposes of God, so that we recognise the reality of judgement (which is happening now in the consequences we bear for our decisions and choices) and the hope of grace.

Ash Wednesday

Yet even now, says the Lord, return to me with all your heart, with fasting, with weeping, and with mourning; rend your hearts and not your clothing. Return to the Lord, your God, for he is gracious and merciful, slow to anger and abounding in steadfast love, and relents from punishing.

(Joel 2:12–13)

Through the process of self-examination, through repentance, through acceptance of our vulnerability and God's generosity, we may attain inner peace. But the message of the Gospel is quite clear: there can be no inner peace without outer justice. We cannot rest content in the face of the world's need for healing and the sense of our complicity in the woundedness of the world.

Is not this the fast that I choose: to loose the bonds of injustice, to undo the thongs of the yoke, to let the oppressed go free, to break every yoke? Is it not to share your bread with the hungry, and bring the homeless poor into your house; when you see the naked, to cover them, and not hide yourself from your own kin? Then your light shall break forth like the dawn, and your healing shall spring forth quickly: your vindicator shall go before you, the glory of the Lord shall be your rearguard. Then you shall call, and the Lord will answer; you shall cry for help, and he will say, Here I am.

(Isaiah 58:6–9)

Prayer

Living God, we confess our faults and admit our frailty; we own our brokenness and recognise the ways we wound our lives, the lives of others, and the life of the world. By your abundant grace forgive us, renew us in mind and in spirit, and enable us to grow in love. Move among us and give us life; with the spirit of freedom sustain us that our worship may be joyful and our witness faithful: in the name of Jesus Christ we pray. Amen.

(Based on the prayers in the morning service in the Iona Abbey Worship Book – 2001 edition)

Norman Shanks

Ash Wednesday

Leader:	Jesus says to his disciples –
A:	Happy are you needy ones:
B:	The kingdom of God is yours.
A:	Happy are you who are hungry:
B:	You will be satisfied.
A:	Happy are you who weep now:
B:	You will be filled with laughter.
A:	Rejected, insulted, happy are you;
B:	Be glad and dance with joy.
Leader:	Jesus said: Take up your cross.
ALL:	WE WILL FOLLOW YOU, O CHRIST,
	INTO THE NEEDS OF THE WORLD;
	INTO THE TRUTH OF OUR LIVES;
	INTO THE PAIN OF OUR HEART;
	INTO THE PRESENCE OF GOD.
	AMEN.

Ashes

– powdery-grey
from keeping on trying
to get a spark from two stones

– streaky black
from relighting a candle
that keeps going out

– soft white
from a fire that burned down to its heart
and kept everyone warm

these are ashes worth wearing

Kathy Galloway

First Sunday
in Lent

Reading:

Luke 4:1–13

Reflection

When we hear that someone is going on retreat, it often conjures up a picture in our mind of escaping from the busyness and stress of everyday life into a kind of pious otherness where we spend all our time talking with God and communing with nature. The very word retreat rather encourages us to this view, suggesting a backing off or getting away from the realities of everyday life.

But the nature of Jesus's wilderness experience challenges us to question and revisit this understanding. The time Jesus spent in the desert, away from the bustle of Galilean life, was far from quiet and serene. It was a period of challenge and temptation, of becoming more aware of God's will, enabling Jesus to counter the easy lure and seductive promises with which Satan tried so hard to snare him.

It is important in all our spiritual journeys to take time out from our everyday busyness to become aware of God's urging in the deepest parts of our being. For many people, spending time away from home in a community, retreat centre or house of welcome can be a very helpful way of quieting our minds and making us receptive to the still small voice within.

But these times of spiritual searching are not periods of disengagement from the world; rather they represent some of the deepest engagement of our lives, when we receive from God the gift of new awareness and learn to see the world around us through the eyes of God.

Once we learn to listen and to become aware, we will find that we continue to hear God's voice amidst life's busyness. Like Jesus we begin to see everyday temptation for what it is and respond to it with the words of God. So as the advertisement falls out of our morning post offering the enticement of instant credit – 'buy now pay later' – we can resist the lure of mammon and of greed, the snare of debt in which so many are trapped for others' profit. As we eat our breakfast, we stop taking our cheap and ready food for granted and begin to ask where it comes from, to think of those who produced it, to see how our choices can make a difference to the lives of others. And so we decide perhaps to drink fair trade coffee and eat local

produce; to let God in as we load our shopping trolleys as well as during times of prayer.

By setting aside time for God, we become more aware of the realities of God's world and the demands of God's justice. And so our heightened experience of an engaged spirituality gives us strength to resist the temptations of wealth, power and prestige and to stand for the way of God in the places and situations where we live and work, love and relate. Not to run away but to stand and be counted. Christ came out of the wilderness to begin his public ministry. We must return from times of retreat to be his pilgrim people in the world.

Prayer

Christ of the wilderness and of the crowded street
Whispering in the desert and shouting in the market
Help us to hear you above temptation's promises
Strengthen us to follow you on the highways of your world.

Helen Boothroyd and Richard Moriarty

Second Sunday in Lent

Reading:

Mark 8:27–28 and Matthew 16:15–17

Reflection

As we sat talking at her bedside, I watched the two nurses who were attending to an elderly woman opposite. 'Come along, Alice. Sit up and eat your meal. We'll take you to the bathroom when you've finished.'

I marvelled at these angels of mercy. They knew everyone on the ward by name. They understood the needs of their patients better than most of them did themselves.

But my friend sadly shook her head. 'No one would have called her Alice before she came here,' she said to me under her breath. 'She was always Mrs Williams – the most respected head teacher the town has ever had.'

Jesus, when you wanted to know
what people were saying about you,
your friends were quick to reply.
There was no shortage of ideas and theories, it seems:
Elijah, John the Baptist,
prophet, teacher, worker of wonders …

But there are different ways of knowing,
different levels and depths.
Peter was more accurate:
'You are the Messiah, the Son of the living God,
the one we are all waiting for,' he said.
Spot on.
Well almost.
Even he hadn't worked out yet
that you had come to give your life
in costly and crucified love.

Different ways of knowing
the people we meet.
To the hospital visitor: one elderly face among many
in a ward of geriatric strangers.
To the nurse: Alice, slightly deaf and slipping down her bed,
to be jollied into recovery from a stroke.
To a fellow patient: Mrs Williams, one-time pillar of the community,
who had nurtured generations of children and teachers.

Two stories. One about you. The other about Mrs A Williams.
They don't quite connect, do they Jesus?
You were, and are, unique.
To know you is to know God:
the deepest kind of knowing.

Yet Mrs A Williams – was she not special too?
Was anyone else quite like her,
with exactly her gifts and commitment,
and her volumes of mystery stories
published secretly under a fictional name?
Was Mrs A Williams not unique –
daughter of God in her own right?

I never knew her. She was not my teacher.
But you are.

Teach me, O Christ.
Teach me to recognise the dignity, the uniqueness,
the divine possibility,
of every living person.

Teach me to take no one for granted,
no friend or stranger,
no crowd or category,
no statistic or stereotype.
Let me never overlook the hidden ones
who yearn for recognition,
and secretly ask, 'Who am I?'

And in that recognition,

in that deepest knowing,
let me encounter you.

And in that encounter
let me, like Peter, be blessed.
For such recognition will hardly be of my own making;
it must be a gift of God.

And in that blessing
let your presence
which I sometimes remember to see in others
also be in me.
And let that which is most truly and uniquely me
be your unfolding within me.
And let me know myself to be
a son, a daughter,
of the living God.

Brian Woodcock

Third Sunday in Lent

Mark 9:2–9

Following Greenpeace estimates and including decommissioning and maintenance costs Trident can be reckoned to cost £45,000 per day since the birth of Christ.

Helen Steven

Cosmic Golgotha

Suppose the material order, as we have argued, is indeed the garment of Christ, the Temple of the Holy Ghost? Suppose the bread and wine, symbols of all creation, are indeed capable of redemption awaiting its Christification? Then what is the atom but the emergent body of Christ?

It was on the mountain top that Jesus was transfigured. He spoke with Moses and Elijah in the Ruach (Hebrew for spirit) world, on the mountain top. He was the At-one-ment, the key to the spiritual and the material: unifying love. And his whole body glistened, the preview of his resurrection body.

Third Sunday in Lent

The Feast of the Transfiguration is August 6th. That is the day when we 'happened' to drop the bomb at Hiroshima. We took his body and we took his blood and we enacted a cosmic Golgotha. We took the key to love and used it for bloody hell.

Nobody noticed. I am not being cheap about other people. I did not notice myself. I was celebrating the Feast of the Transfiguration, in a gown and a cassock, a hood, a stole, white hands, saying with the whole Christian ministry, 'This is my body … this is my blood.'

The while our 'Christian civilisation', without Church protest, made its assertion of the complete divorce between spirit and matter.

One man noticed. When the word came through to Washington of the dropping of the atom bomb – 'Mission accomplished' – Dr Oppenheimer, in large degree in our name its architect, was heard to say, 'Today the world has seen sin.'

Should any reader of this suppose that August 6th, 1945 was the nadir, the lowest point of human disobedience, let us remember that the world potential for perpetrating bloody hell (as 'the lesser of two evils') is now a million times Hiroshima.

George MacLeod

The way to peace

Hiroshima,
Bosnia,
Belfast,
the names slip through our fingers
like bloodstained beads.

As we tell the story,
tell us,
tell us,
tell us,
the way
to peace.

Kosovo,
Nagasaki,
Nuremberg,
still they come, countless numbers:
People hounded, refugees tramping the road
out of hell, into hell.

Where will it stop?
Show us,
show us,

show us,
the way to peace.

Five for sorrow,
ten for joy.
May what has been sown in pain
be reaped in hope.

Kate McIlhagga

Affirmation

(written by Iona Community members after the peaceful demonstration against the Faslane Trident nuclear missile submarine base, February 2001)

WE BELIEVE THAT GOD IS PRESENT
IN THE DARKNESS BEFORE DAWN;
IN THE WAITING AND UNCERTAINTY
WHERE FEAR AND COURAGE JOIN HANDS,
CONFLICT AND CARING LINK ARMS,
AND THE SUN RISES OVER BARBED WIRE.
WE BELIEVE IN A WITH-US GOD
WHO SITS DOWN IN OUR MIDST
TO SHARE OUR HUMANITY.
WE AFFIRM A FAITH

THAT TAKES US BEYOND THE SAFE PLACE:
INTO ACTION, INTO VULNERABILITY
AND INTO THE STREETS.
WE COMMIT OURSELVES TO WORK FOR CHANGE
AND PUT OURSELVES ON THE LINE;
TO BEAR RESPONSIBILITY, TAKE RISKS,
LIVE POWERFULLY AND FACE HUMILIATION;
TO STAND WITH THOSE ON THE EDGE;
TO CHOOSE LIFE
AND BE USED BY THE SPIRIT
FOR GOD'S NEW COMMUNITY OF HOPE.
AMEN.

Fourth Sunday in Lent

Reading:

Mark 9:30–37

Spiritual anorexia

Second-rate disciples are fixated on giving.

But the first task of Christianity is to welcome, to receive. To enjoy without chewing cautiously at the party lest each scrumptious mouthful might be an obligation beyond you to repay.

Receive grace, receive forgiveness, receive people, receive Christ in the stranger, Christ in the child. Christ in yourself for others. Don't starve him by rejecting their kindness. Receive – maybe even receive Christ in yourself for you. Receive the Holy Spirit, the risen Christ will say.

If all you want to do is give, you can't be part of God's family.

Only receive.

Then, maybe, you might be equipped to give.

The Word came to his own, but his own would not receive him. Though the place of honour is the place of receiving. As the servant who opens the door to attend to the guests, Christ worships us with his flesh and blood.

And at the far end of the chain of welcome, only God gives anyway. Because God overflows.

The nature of God was shown us by Jesus to be a community of receiving, living and giving.

Not a hierarchy. Symtheosis.

God the Trinity doesn't run out because God is always stocking up. The 'mathematical' difficulty people have with this aspect of Christianity (three into one won't go) is a smokescreen. It's an excuse for not wrestling with the terrifying idea of collaboration without competition. In God there is no boss. Not even the Father. Jesus's obedience to the Father is not like that. It's the obedience of friendship.

As our toddler son grows up, our equality will become more obvious. In our old age, he may make decisions about us, as for now we do about him. Our hope is that, in between at least, we will be friends. That seemed to be Jesus's hope for the disciples. Special instruction. Quality time.

In God there is no dispute about which person is greatest. Was that what the disciples were really afraid of? Afraid to be affirmed without doing others down? Afraid that they might end up 'rulers' – but with nobody to trample on?

In so many ways, Jesus's teaching turns all our common sense on its head.

As we write this Zam is pregnant. We are hoping to receive a child. We don't know who she or he will be. We have invited – but not created – the growing bump in Zam's abdomen. We are preparing to receive. We expect to be vomited on, to change nappies, to lose sleep. Maybe at three in the morning, with a fistful of poo, the holiness of receiving this task might cross our mind. Maybe we will be too knackered. But who will be the greatest in our family on those sleepless nights?

Prayer

Christ, how we defend and conserve
what is obscure and obsolete!
We evade the point, afraid to ask,
afraid to be seen not to know,
even when your way ahead is clear
but offends common sense.
You can't really mean that anyway!
– So we say.

Christ, don't be too patient with us.
But take us firmly on one side.
Teach us your open secret
To welcome you
in the child, in the vulnerable,
whom the world judges of no importance.
Teach us a greatness
 – outwith pride and respectability –
to turn our world and our selves upside down.

And as we see greatness in each one,
in your love and affirmation
so may we celebrate!
Amen.

David J.M. Coleman and Zam Walker Coleman

Fifth Sunday in Lent

Reading:
Mark 10:32–45

On the road to Jerusalem

On the road to Jerusalem everything is uncertain. It is uncertain for pilgrims travelling there in hope of a faith-renewing experience, but fearful that their visit will be interrupted by bombs and gunfire. It is uncertain for those who live in the surrounding land and travel daily through the roadblocks and barricades with one eye on the wranglings of their political leaders, longing for them to shift, settle, build peace.

And for Jesus and his followers on the road to Jerusalem everything was uncertain, too. They knew that they were walking into conflict. Like migrants approaching a checkpoint knowing their papers are invalid, these travellers could see big trouble ahead.

Did it help that Jesus tried to explain to them what form that trouble would take? Was it any comfort to hear him offer a strange hope of a new beginning after the trauma? Not to James and John, because they had other questions on their minds. If they had to walk this ragged walk, would they find riches at the end of it? If they were to become martyrs, were they guaranteed sainthood later? If they walked beside Jesus through the gunfire, would he keep them beside him in the glory?

Like anybody's children, the sons of Zebedee expected some sort of reward for their labours, a guarantee of security to help them through their struggle, a promise of a certain status in exchange for a certain loyalty. No more and no less than most of us would hope for in this life. No more and no less than we would expect from a loyal and compassionate God. A fair exchange for faith and devotion. As we walk our own Jerusalem roads, we hope to find something safe, secure, rewarding at the end of our journey.

But Christ shocks us by saying (as he did to James and John), 'You don't know what you're asking for.' Christ subverts our hopes by refusing to relinquish the uncertainty. He tells us to put away all expectations of status, security and reward. Instead he holds out his cup for us to drink; he offers us the opportunity to share in the baptism he is baptised with.

On the road to Jerusalem there are no guarantees. Except the guarantee of companionship. Christ invites us to take this ragged road with him and enjoy the riches of his company, to experience sainthood and glory in this present life as we allow ourselves to step along beside him, and we let him lead us through the roadblocks and bullets, the conflicts and pain we encounter along our way. His cup is all we need to nourish us, his baptism all we need to cleanse, renew, refresh us as we go.

Prayer

Help us to accept, O Christ
that our paths may not be smooth
and our journeys may often be risky.

Help us to accept
vulnerability with no promise of security.
Help us to give you
devotion with no promise of reward.

We don't know what we're asking when we ask for these things.
But give us hands to take the cup you hold out to us
– a cup of companionship;
help us gladly immerse ourselves in the baptism you want us to share;
and to so know you on the road with us
that all our anxious thoughts of status, security and reward
wash away,
and we are left with you,
just you,
astonished by your love for us again.

John Davies

Palm Sunday

This is Holy Week. While the hillsides are covered in flowers and people are out gathering herbs to cook, eat or to make into the popular herbal medicines, all around us death and destruction continue and hatred is driving people to carry out the most terrible deeds … In the Middle East everybody has to have a religious label – what they actually believe or practise is irrelevant.

Dr Runa Mackay

Reading:
Luke 19:28–40

Reflection

Palm Sunday in Jerusalem. It's an unforgettable experience – to join the huge procession, led by pipe-bands from the Scout troops in Bethlehem and Beit Jala, thronged with pilgrims from a host of countries, all in bright colours reflecting the spring sunshine and singing in scores of languages – but all uniting in full-throated Hosannas. They walk and swing and sing and wave their palm branches across the top of the Mount of Olives and down the slope through the Garden of Gethsemane and then up towards the narrow Gate into the City. Yes, it's unforgettable, but very different from that first Palm Sunday, when Jesus rode on a donkey's back down that same steep slope, across the Kedron Valley and up into what, for him, was to be a hostile city, a city where shouts of 'Hosanna' would so soon turn to 'Crucify'.

Jerusalem is still a city where hostilities run rampant. On that first Palm Sunday, as he came down the Mount of Olives, Jesus paused and wept over the city: 'Would that even today you knew the things that make for peace! But now they are hid from your eyes.' The 'Al Aqsa Intifada', triggered by the deliberate action of Ariel Sharon, then the leader of the right-wing Likud party and now the Israeli prime minister, is causing heightened enmity between the two communities, Israeli and Palestinian. The innocents are being killed once again – on both sides of the deep divide; atrocities are taking place, with no respite for the bewildered people who long for a measure of security and peace. The international community seems able only to stand aside and watch the spiralling hostility, with no one able to answer the fervent prayer of Jesus for the things that make peace.

There is a way forward. It cannot be based on the love we are commanded to offer our enemies. After all the never-to-be-forgotten atrocities on both sides, that would be asking for the impossible. But there has to be trust. Palestinians and Israelis have so much in common. Their need for a measure of justice towards the other; their longing for that shalom or salaam which are only a syllable away from each other; their need for the land they share to continue to be a place of pilgrimage. The politics of the Holy Land are intractable. After centuries of hostility, it isn't surprising. The basic need is trust. Once there is a basis of trust, there is hope; once there is hope, the talking can be constructive.

God has placed us in a world where different aspirations, however deeply felt, can collide. The lesson we learn from Jerusalem on that first Palm Sunday is that the proud war-horse the Jews were expecting their Messiah to ride turned out to be the humblest of creatures, a donkey. Pride does not inspire trust; humility does. Do I trust the person who is nothing but 'I can do this and that and the other, look at me'? Wouldn't I rather incline to trust the person who says: 'That's a good idea of yours. Maybe you're right. Tell me more.'?

Prayer

*O God our Father, we rejoice in the thrill of Palm Sunday. We see again the bright colours of that triumphant spring day; we hear the shouts of Hosanna; we wave palm branches in unison with the children of Jerusalem. Yet we know that joy can be short-lived, that a crowd is often fickle; and that we are part of the fickleness. Forgive our broken loyalty, we pray. Make us true followers of Jesus, each day of this coming Holy Week, that as we walk the way of his cross, we may commit ourselves all over again to the fashioning of his Kingdom in Jerusalem, in our own communities and across your world. We ask this in the name of Jesus …
AMEN*

Maxwell Craig

Easter Week
Monday

Reading:

Luke 19: 41–48

The spirituality of the city

I to the hills will lift mine eyes.

>   The Psalmist of old

I turn my eyes downtown.

The city – mother and mistress

We lived in Kingston, Jamaica in the early 1980s. The setting of the city is magnificent. It stretches from the edge of the beautiful bay and natural harbour across the coastal plain, rising up gently to the rich green foothills and beyond to the majesty of the great peaks of the famous Blue Mountains.

There are those who would look at this setting – the hotels and high rises, the anonymous, concrete, flat-roofed, single-storey houses built to resist earthquakes and hurricanes, the mile after mile of zinc-roofed shanty town dwellings – and say the city was like a suppurating sore upon the landscape, scarring and disfiguring the natural beauty of the land.

What a diminished existence it must be not to be able to see the beauty of the city; to feel her throbbing heartbeat, to be moved by her great variety of life.

When we came home to Glasgow we were being driven into the city from Edinburgh, past Easterhouse, past Townhead, past Cowcaddens. I thought I was going to cry. I was crying. I was home to the great city which for all her warts had been the mother in whose bosom I was nurtured, where I learned about love, about worth, about dignity, about risk, about faith. I realised that Kingston, to me an exciting mistress for three years, was to her children a mother, the place of nurture for her young and old, her rich and poor, her employed and her unemployed, her overworked ones and her bored and aimless ones.

She is blessed with brown and white and yellow and black children of every shade or mix of complexion. Some of their ancestors came as adventurers. Many came in chains as slaves. Most of the people of Kingston trace their ancestry, through the melting-pot of time, to both slave and adventurer, reflecting the nation's motto: 'Out of many, one people.' Kingston has her honest sons and her dishonest sons; she has her kind daughters and her cruel daughters; she has her fit children and her crippled children. She is their mother.

If we are not moved and courted and touched by a great city where walk together the anxious and the excited, the aggressive and the passive, the healthy and the unhealthy, the talented and the dull – if we are

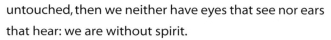

untouched, then we neither have eyes that see nor ears that hear: we are without spirit.

What is true of Kingston is true of Glasgow. When the Psalmist of old speaks in terms of awe and wonder of lifting his eyes to the hills for inspiration and insight, it is with the same wonder and expectancy that I turn my eyes downtown to the heart of the city.

I am a 'war baby', a son of working-class Glasgow, my father a journeyman sheet metal worker in the shipyards, my mother gentle, artistic, but severely asthmatic. I remember the wonder of the city. I remember the bomb shelters in the street; the gas lamps. I remember going the 'messages', at least once going to the shipyard – a place of awesome wonder – with my father.

I remember the 'Left Bookshop' somewhere behind the City Chambers where my dad would take me as he browsed among works of Marx and Engels; and the speakers in Exchange Square on Sunday afternoons, great street theatre before the phrase 'street theatre' was coined. I remember Celtic and Rangers, one of the city's great tribal divisions. I remember the crowds going up Maryhill Road to Firhill to watch Partick Thistle.

One of the greatest wonders was the 'window' of Kemsley House in Hope Street opposite Central

Station, where the *Daily Record* was printed before your very eyes, the great presses rolling out the papers at baffling speed.

I had an auntie who lived in West Graham Street where the mounted police had their stables, and how magnificent they looked as they rode out of the stables in formation in – it seemed – their hundreds. I remember 'the Uni' up on the hill. I remember trams that would go all the way from Maryhill to Ibrox. All these things were part of the wonder of the city. Awesome, like a gigantic cathedral – with life!

For us, the children of the tenements, the 'stair' or 'close' was the defining arena of our upbringing. Although the best part of half a century has elapsed, if I shut my eyes I can still picture those who lived up our stair. I remember the first time my wee brother and I were allowed to go out guisin' at Halloween and first-footing at New Year, we were told, 'You can go up the stair, but not out the close.' The stair was a place of safety and up that stair not only would every adult assume the right to chastise any child that lived up the stair, they would also take responsibility if a child was in trouble, or was locked out because their mother wasn't home. I think I had skint knees soothed by half the adults up our stair and my ears skited by the other half!

Is it only in the rosy glow of hindsight that this seems a model of community? I think not! If spirituality is that which invigorates, which underlines purpose, worth, dignity and belonging, it is surely to be found in the city if only we have eyes to see and ears to hear.

The house, the stair, the school: this was the cradle of discipline and protection from which we, the children of the tenements, ventured out into the big world of risk and competition, of adult relationships and the workplace.

The city – place of discovery

I was driving back to Dundee, where I now live, across the Tay Road Bridge one stormy November evening as dusk was approaching. The sky about the city was leaden, the wind was whipping up the river, the rain was lashing down. Between the dark skies and the turbulent waters the city throbbed with life, her lights sparkling, her high-rises and church spires reaching up to touch the dark skies. Nature, impressive in her raw fury; the city, undaunted, sparkling with life. Human creativity and the creation of God, one seamless garment, as George MacLeod used to argue about the sacred and the secular.

As the city of Dundee emerged from the traumas of the demise of the three Js (jute, jam and journalism) for which she was famous, the city's leaders adopted the slogan 'Dundee, City of Discovery'. The *RRS Discovery*, built in Dundee, is the ship whose epic voyage under the command of Captain Scott to the Antarctic ended in despair and disaster, for not only did Scott die on the expedition, he was beaten to the South Pole by the Norwegian Amundsson.

Adopting the ship as the centrepiece of the City of Discovery Campaign is a sign of having the courage to embrace the reality of life. George MacLeod in his prayer 'The whole earth shall cry glory' says:

> *But creation is not enough.*
> *Always in the beauty, the foreshadowing of death.*
> *The lambs frolicking careless, so soon to be led off to slaughter.*
> *Nature red and scarred as well as lush and green.*
> *In the garden also; always the thorn.*
> *Creation is not enough!*

Surely, for those who have ears to hear, the city echoes back:

> *Creation is not enough;*
> *Always in the midst of enterprise and innovation,*

the cancer of self and sectional interest.
Children full of life and expectation,
soon to be thrown on the scrapheap of disadvantage.
The city dark, destructive and violent
as well as full of generosity and love.

Surely those who have eyes to see, see the divisions we create: Bearsden and Bridgeton; Croftfoot and Castlemilk; Cramond and Craigmillar; Monifieth and Mid-Craigie. We know we cannot create ghettos of privilege without creating ghettos of poverty. For those with ears to hear, the voice of Jesus crying over Jerusalem still echoes across the centuries – 'How I wanted to gather all your people like a hen gathers her chicks under her wing, but you would not let me.'

George MacLeod continues:

Almighty God, Redeemer:
the sap of life in our bones and being is yours,
lifting us to ecstasy.

The city echoes back:

Redemption and renewal are ever with us, indivisible from creation.

In the church, on a wedding day, they talk of the love that shall cause a man to leave his mother and father and be joined to his wife and they too shall be one flesh. The modern city talks about the mystery of the mixing of the genes that gives each new generation its uniqueness. Whilst almost every minute of the day new life is being born in the great maternity hospitals, so too, in urban crematoria, thanks are given minute by minute for the lives that have brought us, in the cities, to where we are now.

Almighty God, Redeemer,
the sap of life in our city bones and being is yours,
and we can see it and feel it on the grand scale
lifting us to ecstasy.

With death and decay in our nostrils, with renewal and redemption tangible, the living spirit of the city embraces us, and we who are the children of the city feel our chests swell. Thanks be to God!

Erik Cramb

Weeping for cities and working for justice

The pain of the city is complex. The suffering that cripples our inner cities is often the pain of lifetimes and generations. The pain of individuals is bound up with the pain of the whole community. A battered child is all too often the child of parents who were, in their turn, battered by their parents. When a child is killed on a busy road that runs through a housing estate, or an old person dies of hypothermia because they cannot afford to heat an all-electric flat, the whole community suffers. The community suffers because all their children and all their pensioners are at risk, and will continue to be at risk until there is a change.

And how do I pray for healing for this community? When I begin to pray for individuals I meet, I find myself praying and acting for the whole community. I cannot pray for an old person with bronchitis if I do not also put pressure on a council or a landlord who is responsible for the damp and substandard housing that is the root cause of the illness.

How can I pray for those who are lonely, old and disabled if I do not take time to visit them and, at the same time, ask why there is so little funding to provide sheltered accommodation and to staff daycentres? I cannot pray for families living in tower-blocks, whose relationships are at break-ing-point, and whose children are distressed, if I do not raise questions about the way government and local authorities allocate housing stock and fund playspace and nursery provision.

I cannot pray for young people in prison if I do not look for ways to relieve the boredom of unemployment, the pressure of advertising, the high cost of accommodation and the ready availability of drugs that have combined to destroy their liberty. I cannot pray for people who are poor in my community, or for that matter for people who are hungry, oppressed and poor anywhere in the world, if I do not challenge the way that my country's government spends its resources.

I say I cannot pray. What I mean is that I cannot pray for the healing of others with integrity without also acting on my prayers. If I am blind to the sources of injustice around me, and divorce the needs of an individual from the pain of a whole community, my prayers for healing are non-sense and bear no resemblance to the good news of the gospel ...

Jesus, you wept for the city you loved – in your words and actions the oppressed found justice and the angry found release ...

(prayer heading used on Iona)

Weeping for cities and working for justice is rarely dramatic or sensational. It is not an activity that brings instantaneous results. The suffering of a dispossessed community, in Britain or anywhere else in the world, has no easy solutions. For healing and justice to occur there needs to be change – change in values and attitudes; change in political policies and social conditions. And change for those in need means change for everyone, and none of us change easily.

When we pray for the healing of those around us, are we willing to live out the implications of our prayers?

Jesus, teach us how to pray.

Ruth Burgess

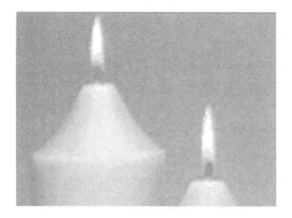

Prayer

Visionary God, architect
of heaven and earth,
unless we build in partnership with you we labour in vain

Help us work to create cities
modelled more faithfully
on the plan of your Kingdom –

Communities where children are respected and encouraged
where young people can express themselves creatively
where the experience of old people is called on
where the insights and gifts of all God's people are fully realised
where shared gardens and plots bloom in once derelict places

Easter Week Monday

where all cultures and traditions are honoured and celebrated
on soulful, carnival streets
where gay couples can dance to the beat of their hearts
homeless people are received with loving arms and open borders
news vendors cry Hosanna!
All are fed and loved and set free ...

O God, our maker, open our eyes to new possibilities and perspectives,
organisations and projects, structures and outlooks ...

Help us to rebuild the walls of Jerusalem:

to break down the barriers in ourselves that
prevent us from reaching out to neighbours and making peace;
to rebuild communities based on understanding and justice,
illuminated with the true light of Christ.
Amen

Neil Paynter

Easter Week
Tuesday

Reading:

Mark 11:12–19

Too often we are the money changers:
giving short change in spiritual things
to many who seek the true coin:
making the Church an institute
when you want it to be a chaos of uncalculating love.

George MacLeod

Ducks, hens and a black goat

It was Harvest Festival. The sun was slowly sinking as we came near the small village – 'cow dust' time – when everything across the land seems still, and the great heat of the day has passed. As we entered the village in the gathering darkness, we were greeted by a real sense of celebration. The little church, brightly lit up against the surrounding darkness, was like a bright star in a dark sky. Although the church was lit up by a few electric bulbs, it was the rows of candles on all the windows which added to the magic. The flames of these candles were blowing gently in the evening breeze reminding us of the symbol of light which is both at the heart of the Christian gospel and deep within the ancient spiritual traditions of Hinduism. Everywhere there were children, most of them singing Tamil songs with great enthusiasm. As we approached the church, several of the local women welcomed us with a traditional dance. They danced with their whole being, and with deep devotion. And in the simple beauty of their movements, a thousand words were spoken.

The scene inside the church would be hard to describe. Every square inch was taken up with people: old men, young men; old women, young women; youths and children and tiny babies, and any space that was left over was occupied by hens, ducks, a jumping goat, vegetables, fruit, baskets of rice and many other things from the village fields. The whole place seemed to be praising the Creator, not least a large cockerel perched on a bag of paddy and gazing earnestly at a picture of Christ hanging behind the Communion table. Another hen almost caught fire during the second hymn as it squeezed up against a candle on the window ledge. Five ducks sat under my stool and just as we began a rather long prayer, one of them jumped onto the paddy and began to have supper.

As the service went on, the young children began to go to sleep one by one. Soon there were many little figures spread across the floor. Sometimes the mothers and grandmothers dozed lightly with them, but when we sang the familiar Tamil lyrics all were awake and the music could be heard in the surrounding villages. The whole church was alive with music and it drifted out across the moonlit fields, over the tall palm trees and down to the tank where the buffaloes rested.

After the service was over, we shared with a village family in their evening meal. Their small hut was full of warmth, love and welcome. Then we returned to the church where the elders were auctioning the hens, the ducks, the vegetables and the paddy for church funds. There was a great deal of laughter and much noise. It was very late when the auction ended, but by now no one was tired.

Soon we started on our homeward journey. But we were returning with more than we had come with, for we had purchased some of the ducks at the auction. We said our farewells and headed down the mud road. Above us the stars were shining over the empty fields and the night was still and very silent; a deep stillness. Within a few minutes we could no longer hear the singing and the laughter and the shouts of children. The Harvest Festival was over for another year.

Yet the joy and fellowship of that evening would not be forgotten, for in that poor village we had experienced the riches of Christ.

Peter Millar

Peacemakers in a changing world

Gandhi said, 'To refuse to struggle against the evil of the world is to surrender your humanity, to struggle against the evil of the world with the weapons of the evil-doer is to enter into your humanity, to struggle against the evil of the world with the weapons of God is to enter into your divinity.'

It is a hard fact of life that as Christians we are called upon to be prophetic, to be prepared to resist. 'Resist not evil with evil, but rather overcome evil with good.' I feel that many of us in the church shy away from confrontation. It's not nice – most of us would rather be gentle, non-confrontational, peaceful, calm. That is assuredly not the calling of the church: we must be disciples, prophetic, difficult, prepared to 'speak truth to power', make ourselves unpopular. 'Without fear, happy, and always in trouble.'

So what are the powers we are called to confront in our rapidly changing world?

Poverty, homelessness, degradation of the human spirit, all that denies the abundant life of Christ must be resisted in practical ways if we are truly seeking peace based on justice. Take this example which certainly gave me hope. A group of young Christian activists occupied a derelict children's hospital in London and opened it up to two hundred homeless people. The organisers were jailed but two hundred desperate people had won the right to housing …

As we plunge deeper into the market economy, we are called to question ever more keenly our economic structures. When Jesus overturned the tables in the Temple, he was challenging the economic pillars of Judaic society and ecclesiastical complicity. Are we prepared to overturn the tables?

Helen Steven

Easter Week Tuesday

Prayer

Jesus, help us to create churches
with your passion and light planted at the heart

Churches where we are prepared to address injustice and
where 'in a gesture a thousand words are spoken'

Challenging, prophetic churches possessing
a generous, rich fund of warmth and love and
welcome and real celebration.

Christ, light and life of the world,
bless your Church with the grace and power
to flourish and bear fruit;
the courage and faith
to grow rooted in your gospel
and in the grassroots of community.
Amen

Neil Paynter

Easter Week Wednesday

Reading:
Matthew 26:1–16

Reflection

When it comes to money, it's open season. Anyone can tell you how to spend your money – the less you have, the more they feel obliged to let you know where you're going wrong.

Saving your money – now that's a Good Thing. Of course, it's only a Good Thing as long as you save it for the right reasons. Saving it to splurge, like the woman who spent her hard-earned pennies on expensive perfume and poured the perfume over Jesus's feet – well, it's true what Jesus said, 'What was done is told in remembrance of her', but do we approve? It's easy, in hindsight – the gospel writers can add their own gloss, and we can see her as a prophet – but if I do the same kind of thing today, I will probably meet the same sort of response.

I don't suppose she was a wealthy woman. Maybe she saved a few pennies from produce sold at market. Maybe the precious ointment was kept strictly to anoint family members after death.

So she risked breaking a lot of rules and getting on the wrong side of quite a few people. An ordinary woman, breaking into the house of a respectable man, wasting her precious gift on a disturbing itinerant preacher, doing something so personal, so intimate – well, there's no salvation for a woman like that.

Maybe you know what she felt like. Playing a 'Poverty Trap' game in a group some years later, I recalled my time as a single parent. In the game of life, I broke all the rules – if I only had a few pounds left, I'd spend it on my child's birthday present before paying the rent. The council could wait; my child needed to be assured of my love – now. I'd do the same today – bills can wait, but the people I love will never go without.

The same extravagant response to God's love has moved people over the centuries to build cathedrals, churches, mosques, temples and synagogues, and to cover those who lead worship, and the buildings themselves, in gorgeous finery. Some traditions argue against splendour in building and fabric, as well as in music – but the parallel between costly and tangible giving to a loved one and to the God we love and worship has endured for many thousands of years. One woman's gesture of love turns out to be part of a humanising instinct, to show love through gifts we can touch, taste, smell, see or hear.

Thank God for the woman whose act of love we will always remember.

Prayer

Thank God for all those who make extravagant gestures of love before it is too late. Pray for the wisdom to know when such sacrifice is called for – to know that the value of money is what it can do, not what it is. Pray for the grace to take risks, to give without counting the cost, not to worry about security, to trust God's promise. Pray for the humility to know that one person's extravagance may be another's sacrificial gift, another's wisdom. Pray for the grace to believe that security lies not in stocks and bonds and bank balances, but in the God who responds to a generous spirit. Amen

Anna Briggs

Maundy Thursday

Judas: reflections on Matthew 26:17–25

I have known betrayal. My best friend Fiona approached me in the playground. She had news for me. My 'boyfriend', John, had sent her to tell me that he was no longer my 'boyfriend'. He was Fiona's. Rejection was covered by twelve-year-old nonchalance.

I have known betrayal. Many years of training for a career of my dreams, to be told that the vision that had been nurtured in me was to be shelved: anger welled up in me, and defiance too.

I have known these betrayals. But I have not known the nearness of death when a 'friend' turns into a fatal enemy. I have not known the lure of a 'wise' one's invitation as it turns into abuse, scorn, harm. I have not known the humiliation of a people scorned and stigmatised.

Have you known betrayal?

And have you known what it is to be a betrayer? Have you known what it is wilfully to plan to injure, hurt, abuse one you care for? Have you known the power you have to turn kind words into sneers and sniggers, into condemnations, into deathly, deadly threats of violence and worse? Have you glimpsed the turmoil, the remorse, or perhaps the glow and the glory that some betrayers must feel beyond their action?

As betrayer and as betrayed, Judas is 'everyperson' for us.

Maundy Thursday

I

I live in the Shadowlands

the wrecker and
the wreaker of havoc
the first denier
the immovable stone

translucent only to him
who had eyes to see beyond seeing
(and who, I now know, sees beyond all knowing).

I am the 'altar' ego,
the 'inn'-dweller
inhabiting an intimate space in each soul – your landscape –
surely alert, alive,
to the daily decisions
and whimsical choices
showing themselves
at every turn
(as is my companion – the light of truth and openness).

Maundy Thursday

I am a free-thinker and free-mover –
I am no helpless victim
destined for a superimposed fate
I am a player in the game of freedom
choice
free-will
(free-gift?)

II

And my offence?
my great transgression?

In the presence of the one
who was to ride, unmasked, to his death,
to die, naked,
I clung to my masks and to my garments;
I hung on to the shimmering identity
I so longed for.

I know the security
and the safety in the hiding,

Maundy Thursday

the sometimes necessary clinging
– hanging on (is this familiar to you too?)

But I did not know how,
when or whether to let go,
to bare myself
to stand naked before the gift and giver.

I was taken in, deceived,
betrayed
by the self-deception:
just like any of us …

I am the betrayer
I am the betrayed.

Words of prayer

Sweet Jesus, forgive us when we have been betrayers –
when we have colluded with the powers of evil to hurt others,
to harm the ones we care about.

Sweet Jesus, loving Christ,
cradle us when we have been betrayed –
rock us in your soft arms –
arms that have known hurt beyond our imagining.

Maundy Thursday

Hold us secure to your bosom, caressing the pain and the fear,
the guilt and the anger until it lifts like a gentle cloud from our souls
and we can breathe once more.

This we ask in your name,
Amen

Ruth Harvey

Maundy Thursday

Evening

Reading:
Matthew 26:36–46

A room

This is a big room really. It's because there are six beds. It's because there are six beds that it looks small. I start at the back and with my cart – diapers, creams, lotions, baby powder – work my way up, from bed to bed. Rouse the old men gently and get them ready for the long day – wash, dress, transfer to wheelchair.

There is Gordon. He had to flee his home town out East after returning from the war. 'It was just too much,' he told me one morning as I was giving him a quick bed bath, the curtain drawn around us. Without Gordon's knowledge, someone in a local recruiting office had used his eager face on a local poster. And when he landed, victorious and whole, all the mothers who had lost sons, and all the girls and wives who had lost lovers descended on him like a pack. Blamed him. Took their anger out on young Gordon. On the streets the townspeople called him a Judas. Asked him straight out: 'So, where's your thirty pieces of silver, Gord?' Threw dirty pennies at this feet.

There is Mr Eliot. He was a graduate student in philosophy at the University of Toronto. Then wrote several novels, later in life, children's books. But he cannot see well enough now – almost not at all. His cataracts are ripe but the doctors don't think it's worth operating.

He's messed his bed again. He says he's sorry. I tell him it's all right, not to worry about it. As I change the bed I change the subject, telling him that I'm a writer, too. We sit and talk about authors. We chat about Somerset Maugham and agree that *Of Human Bondage* was his most mature. He touches my face with his cold fingertips. Then smiles. 'You have a beard, too. Can't you sit and talk with me a while longer?' I explain that I have to move on.

'Could you come back later, after you're finished?'

I explain that I have been up all night. And that I really must go home. But maybe some other time. For sure some other time.

There is Mr Finny. There's a car on the roof, he says. Horses thundering in the yard. In the war he defused mines – 60 cents a day. He takes me aside and reports, whispering hoarsely, that guns are pointing at us from out of the wall sockets. Then he squints suspiciously at my cart. He is convinced there's a bomb buried beneath the heap of bleached blankets. Won't get up until I prove all is safe. Until I've defused it. He'll explain to me how. 'Now go slow boy. Go slow.'

There is Mr Hamilton. Years ago he lost his legs due to diabetes and drinking. Due to neglect. Now his stomach is swollen. He's pregnant with bile. He tells

Maundy Thursday

me they're admitting him for tests tomorrow and thanks me for being so patient with him last night. For mopping his burning brow with a cool cloth. For mopping up when he was sick. The head nurse takes me aside and whispers they suspect stomach cancer. Mr Hamilton has drunk himself to death and won't be here when I come back next week. I say goodbye. Wish him luck. 'Hang in there, you salty old mariner,' I call. He laughs. It hurts him to laugh now. 'Ouch, ya thanks, see ya skipper.'

This bed is empty. Ron Shepherd died last week. He kept calling for me in the night. When I finally came, he'd forgotten what he wanted. I offered him a sip of cool water. He gulped it greedily through the plastic straw. The moment I stepped out of the room he'd bellow again, madly sounding the call buzzer safety-pinned to his pillow. Finally, I told him off. Finally, I ignored him. I had no idea how bad he was. No idea death was stalking him when I was sitting down the hall reading the newspaper.

Jack is sleeping. He's always sleeping now. It's less painful. We used to talk a little. About his son out in Vancouver. Now he only wakes for his pills. Stricken with a rare form of muscular dystrophy, his two sets of ribs stick up like sharp fins threatening to pierce through his thin skin. It's as if he'd swallowed sharks. I turn him to change his pad. He doesn't wake. I see black blood beginning to leak. I see thick blood beginning to flow. I call a nurse. She calls a doctor.

I leave the room with six beds thinking this is only one room in a world full of rooms.

The world itself like one big, cramped room.

Neil Paynter

Maundy Thursday

Gethsemane prayer

Jesus, our brother,
once you knelt sleepless
in the darkness of a garden
alone
and wept and prayed,
sweating, bleeding,
with the pain of powerlessness
with the strain of waiting.
An angel offered you strength –
but it was a bitter cup.

We pray for all
who wake tonight
waiting, agonising,
anxious and afraid,
while others sleep:
for those who sweat
and bleed, and weep alone.
If it is not possible
for their cup to be taken away –
then may they know your presence
kneeling at their side.

Amen

Jan Sutch Pickard

Maundy Thursday

Once more

Once more
to see a snowdrop
to smell the sea
once more
once more
to hold the child
to be a wordsmith
once more
once more
to dance a reel
dive into a pool
once more
once more
once more, O Lord
once more.

Kate McIlhagga

Good Friday

Reading:
Mark 15:1–15

I have come to understand that my fear of embracing the enormity of my own fragility and capacity for violence and corruption, coupled with a longing for the creative freedom which such an embrace could bring, attracts me to work in HM Prison whatever other more acceptable labels I have given my work there …

The men in prison where I draw, relate and teach German have honoured me with the gift of their vulnerability. Many of them are able to discern the true freedom that comes when one is stripped of all status, and it is thus that they can teach me something about the meaning of spiritual poverty. In coming to serve the poor, so to speak, I am discovering … that I am poor.

Joyce Gunn Cairns

Good Friday

Prison quartet

1. *Inside*

> Like a sheepfold
> the high wall gathers all in –
> the loud and the subdued,
> the lost sheep
> and the easily led.
>
> Instead of drystone and hurdles
> there are concrete and wire,
> barred gates, locks, curfews, IDs –
> a claustrophobic and complete world.
>
> And in its long corridors
> there are people like you and me,
> caught in patterns of life, rituals
> alien and alienating to those outside.
>
> Only a few have keys.
> Who would be a shepherd in this fold?

2. *Nurse*

> She glows
> like an aconite
> in the midwinter cold,
> amid corridors

of barren concrete,
and her conversation
is about weddings,
chapel teas, family jokes
and the fact (no joking now)
that she loves her job.

3. *Keys*

Seven years
for a crime against property,
not people. Seven years
in a place utterly unlike
all he has known before,
among angry strangers.
After seven years
will he be the same person?
How can he hold on
to his own worth?
How unlock reality in this alien place?
His fingers touch the keys
of the chapel piano.
Music is welling up
from the depth of his being:
it cannot be contained by bars
it dances out of bounds.

Good Friday

4. *Bird*

One day,
said the chaplain,
a seagull flew
into the razor wire
on the prison wall
and hung there impaled,
but still alive.
Any moment it would beat its wings,
to fly to freedom,
and, in doing so, tear itself to pieces.
All over the prison
men stopped what they were doing
and watched in horror.
The warders said
'Get it down, get it down.'
They fetched a ladder
and leaned it against the wire.
'You go,' they said. 'You're the chaplain.'
And he climbed the ladder
until he could touch
the white feathers stained with blood.
The bird watched him with a mad eye,
huge and dangerous in its pain.
He couldn't lift it clear of the wire.

Good Friday

Over the wall was the world –
but the dying bird filled the horizons.
He came down to earth again
with blood on his hands.
The bird died
and the hard men wept.

Jan Sutch Pickard

Good Friday

Crucified by envy

But Pilate answered them, saying, Will ye that I release unto you the King of the Jews? For he knew that the chief priests had delivered him for envy ... And they cried out again, Crucify him ... (Mark 15:9,10,13)

I am like the chief priests: I have known the destructive power of envy of others all too frequently, decades of its foul grip. Nowadays as a woman and an artist trying to speak my truth and discovering great meaning in that struggle as well as affirmation from others, I find myself on the receiving end of envy. Envy presumes that the envied object is enjoying a state of bliss. This presumption is, I imagine, infallibly inaccurate. It is certainly not an accurate description of my inner world. As the self-confessed Son of God, Jesus was, according to the aforesaid presumption, enjoying a state of bliss par excellence. And Envy, raging at the good fortune of another, must destroy. So they battered him to a bloody, lacerating death.

My risk-taking, in comparison to Jesus's, pales into insignificance. Nevertheless I am trying to speak my truth, and as a result I suffer at times from the pain and rejection of others' envy. This dialogue – my struggle to speak my truth, and the envy this elicits – takes its most visible form, literally and metaphorically, in relation to my work as an artist. My work is not decorative, but it is real. Giles Sutherland, art critic with *The Times*, said of my works exhibited in the Scottish National Portrait Gallery, that they 'are deeply felt studies of the inner self, displaying a soul-searching spirituality and a searing, painful honesty in equal measure' (*The Times*, March 2001). In speaking my truth about the very special gifts that God has given me, the

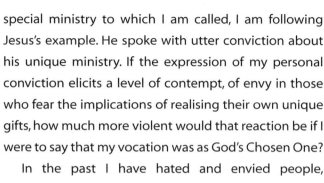

special ministry to which I am called, I am following Jesus's example. He spoke with utter conviction about his unique ministry. If the expression of my personal conviction elicits a level of contempt, of envy in those who fear the implications of realising their own unique gifts, how much more violent would that reaction be if I were to say that my vocation was as God's Chosen One?

In the past I have hated and envied people, especially women, who have spoken their truth, and whose God-given creativity has flowered as a result. Now that I am ranking myself with them, and my vocation deepens and is confirmed as a result, I am on the receiving end of the very hostility which I once meted out. Now that I have tasted something of the pain, and the creativity, of self-disclosure, how would I react to a man meeting me in the street and telling me that he was the Christ, the son of God? I would not question the validity of his claim. I am confident about that. I know through much salutary experience that Christ comes indeed often in the stranger's guise. But would I follow him, stand beside him in solidarity if he were tortured and crucified? Alas, I fear not. How easy it is to applaud his ministry in retrospect. But if I had been there, on that day, mingling with the crowd baying for his blood? And if, like Peter, I had been identified as one of his friends? And if admission of this friendship put my skin and that of my dear ones at risk?

And the crowd's vicious insistence on a scapegoat is only half the story. Because Jesus spoke not one word in his defence. 'And the chief priests accused him of many things: but he answered nothing' (Mark 15:3). Nothing. Why did he speak not one word? What are we to understand from his silence? My own belief is that Jesus – whatever else he was or is, Son of God, Messiah – was the incarnation of a Soul evolved to heights beyond our comprehension, who had, through aeons of self-searching and self-disclosure, become detached from any need for self-justification, whether the offence against him was misunderstanding and rejection, or the threat of torture and death. This is my understanding of his stature. And his silence speaks with the eloquence of authority vested in that stature.

Joyce Gunn Cairns

Simon carries the cross

Reading: Mark 15:21–22 (Good News Bible)

On the way they met a man named Simon, who was coming into the city from the country, and the soldiers forced him to carry Jesus' cross. (Simon was from Cyrene and was the father of Alexander and Rufus.) They took Jesus to a place called Golgotha, which means 'The Place of the Skull'.

The door of Sam's room had been left open by the nurses. His family's distress was obvious – his wife holding his hand, his daughter with her arm round her mum, his son staring out of the open window – as they waited for Sam to die. I wanted to go in and meet this family in their sorrow. But I had nothing to offer, no clever words to say. I only glanced into the room as I passed, a spectator of their pain and grief.

It could not and would not last. Eventually, I felt compelled to go in. I was scared, ill-equipped, tongue-tied, out of my depth. But for a moment or two, and on two or three other occasions throughout the day, I offered what I could – a stumbling word, a shared silence, a comforting touch – each time overwhelmed by the pain of it all and my uselessness to make it any different.

Sam died that night. Next morning, the door of his room was still open. But there was no patient or distressed family, only the empty bed and the stillness of the aftermath of death. I was relieved it was over for them – but also for me, for I needed no longer be burdened by the weight of my inadequacy.

Good Friday

Later that morning, the family came to collect Sam's belongings and the death certificate – and asked to see me, to say thank you for my help during yesterday. My help? I murmured some words of protest. But Sam's wife persisted: 'No, you did good yesterday. All the family have said so, because you came into the room – and I know how hard that was for you.'

'You came into the room – and I know how hard that was.' The ultimate had not been possible – I could not stop the journey to death. My own inadequacies had been transparent – I would rather have been anywhere than be a part of the pain and sorrow. But with the compulsion to go in and the fearfulness of being there, in the transition from spectator to participant, something good – of God – had taken place.

Simon, too, looked through a wide-open door and witnessed a journey to death. And he too – coming up from Cyrene, minding his own business, maybe wishing he was back with Alexander and Rufus – was forced to enter the drama. What good could he possibly do as he carried Christ's burden? Could he make the ultimate difference? Could he stop the crucifixion? From distant spectator to reluctant participant carrying a cross – what good was there in this? The good is God saying 'Thank you, Simon,' for being there when you were needed and others had turned away.

When the ultimate is beyond you, but you still step over the threshold into the distress and pain, you are Simon for Christ, and God says 'Thank you' for your healing presence.

When you stop walking by with old excuses of better things to do, but are forced into the drama, you are Simon on the road to Golgotha, and God says 'Thank you' for being involved.

When you cease being a spectator but become a participant, bearing that painful burden for a few, stumbling steps, you are Simon carrying the cross of Christ, and God says 'Thank you' for your willing shoulder.

When you withdraw, consumed by your inadequacy, you are Simon being Simon, until there is another drama to enter, another threshold to cross, and another cross to carry, with God saying 'Thank you' for learning that your love makes a diference.

Prayer

God who knows my frailties, forgive my self-doubt and uncertainty when I am content from a distance to watch others' pain.

God who calls my name, even when I am reluctant, forgive my resistance and my fear of being overwhelmed by the task you compel me to take on.

God who offers me the cross, a burden too great for me to carry, help me be a willing participant on a journey I can neither understand nor change.

God who believes in me, help me to go on believing that you take the little I have offered and use it to make a difference.

God who knows me and calls me, who burdens me and believes in me, help me to hear your voice of thanks, and be ready to serve again.

Tom Gordon

Good Friday

The sixth hour

Reading:
John 19:14–30

… I simply argue that the cross be raised again at the centre of the market place as well as on the steeple of the church. I am recovering the claim that Jesus was not crucified in a cathedral between two candles, but on a cross between two thieves; on the town garbage heap; at a crossroad so cosmopolitan that they had to write his title in Hebrew and in Latin and in Greek (or shall we say in English, Xhosa and in Afrikaans?) at the kind of place where cynics talk smut, and thieves curse, and soldiers gamble.

Because that is where he died. And that is what he died about …

George MacLeod

Prayer of the crucified

(Mark 15:34)

(to be shared by several voices: below is just one possibility)

A   My God, my God
Why have you forsaken me?
Father, mother
look what is happening to your child.
Loving God
how can you let this happen to any of your children?

B   Look at these feet:
they walked the dusty roads
they walked into so many homes
of neighbours, strangers, lonely people.
These feet danced at weddings
and went to the graveyard
to bring back Lazarus.
They were soothed with ointment
by a woman no one else wanted to touch.
And now they are nailed to the cross
with iron nails
forced through skin, sinew and bone
into splintering wood.
These feet cannot walk in your world any more.
My God, why?

Good Friday

C   The woman in a wheelchair after an accident,

A   the man in detention without trial,

C   the elderly victim of a stroke, in a hospital bed,

A   the child labourer tethered in a back room of a slum
      in a far away country, sold by her parents.

C   Cut off from others,

A   unable to walk away from their problems,

C   disabled,

A   pinned down by pain

All   My God, why?

B   Look at these hands:
      they made tables, tools, toys
      in the carpenter's workshop;
      they reached out in love
      to people who were in pain, outsiders,
      and healed and helped them;
      they plucked ears of corn,
      they drew patterns in the sand;
      they washed tired feet,
      they broke bread to share among friends.
      And now they are broken,
      they are caked with dirt and blood,
      they are pierced through the palm
      with cruel nails.

These fingers curl and stretch in agony.
There is nothing else they can do.
My God, why?

C   Look at the unwanted old woman, who sits with hands in lap,

A   the unemployed man, hands hanging idle,

C   the people watching famine victims
      – how can they lift a hand to help? –

A   the person suffering from AIDS
      who has reached a point of weakness
      when he can do nothing for himself:

C   skilled, caring, creative hands – helpless.

All   My God, why?

B   Look at this head:
      It used to turn
      to the single voice in the crowd,
      the outsider.
      It bent
      to be alongside and listen to children.
      It fell asleep on a pillow
      in the bows of a boat in a big storm,
      trusting in God.
      Long ago it fell asleep
      on a mother's breast.
      Now it is restless

Good Friday

on the rough wood of the cross
with an unbelieving slogan pinned above,
with a mocking crown of thorns
pressed down on the tender skin
of the forehead,
so that blood
runs into the eyes, already blinded
with tears of pain
My God, why?

A   Look at the person suffering from migraine,
       the inescapable pain
       that will not let you think or act;
C   those who wear the thorny crown
       of responsibilities;
A   those sleepless with worry, for a loved one far away,
       for the future, for what path to choose;
C   the confused, who cannot choose:
       who weep without knowing why.
All   My God, why?

B   Look at this body:
       It carried the cross to this place
       and the ones who will carry it from here to the tomb
       include the woman who, years ago,
       carried the child in her womb.

This body lived with family and friends –
at home here –
was down to earth, needed food, drink,
grew tired, felt pity, anger, joy, surprise
and now feels only pain,
despair – and pain
thirst – and pain.
It is tortured by the cross;
it cannot see further than the cross;
it becomes one with the cross;
it is pain.
My God, why?

A   Look at the man, the woman, tortured in gaols
     of a dozen countries, in our world.
C   Look at the children, growing up under the threat
     of big guns, which we have made.
A   Look at the prisoner on the rooftop,
     battered by noise, baffled by doubts
     no longer knowing why he is there – in our system.
C   Look at the homeless, growing in number,
     living rejected in our city.
A   Look at the human being, devoured by cancer,
     eaten up with pain
     which we cannot cure – our pain.

Good Friday

C   Look at this woman
      rejected by one that she loves;

A   Look at this man – a figure of fun;

C   Look at this heart pierced with pain – our pain.

All   My God, why?

B   Our God
      have you forsaken us?
      or are you there,
      sharing our suffering,
      on the cross?

Jan Sutch Pickard

Easter Week
Saturday

Reading:

Luke 23: 50–56

The work of grief

To lose someone you love is the most painful, the most all-absorbing event. It feels as though the strong emotions of grief will swamp, devour and drown you. 'No one told me grief could be so much like fear,' was how C.S. Lewis experienced it. 'My anger threatened to engulf me. I felt numb. I felt nothing. I felt guilty because I felt nothing. People tell me they know how I feel. How can they know how I feel? Only I can know that. I feel … everything and nothing.'

Gradually over days, weeks, months, years, the person who has been bereaved, who has had their loved one snatched from them, is able to weave a tapestry of hope from all these feelings. You don't know that that is what it is at the time. Numbness and shock interweave with denial and anger. Grief and pain form dark threads overlaid by occasional flashes of remembered joy. Grief work is hard. It is like an inexperienced knitter dropping stitches, having to go back to stage one and start again. Looking for the person who has died, seeing them on a bus, imagining you hear their voice, raises momentary hope. It has all been a bad dream. Then realisation brings fear of madness. Hatred is akin to love and, just as we all have mixed feelings about those we love, we will have mixed feelings about those who have died: How dare he go away and leave me with all this? I feel so guilty feeling the way I do about her.

The garment of grief woven from fear and anger, denial and pain, sadness and tiredness becomes a familiar scarf: something to wrap around you; something for comfort. One day you forget to put it on. You forget for an hour – or even two. Then, as usual, when you wake up it all comes flooding back. Everyone is different, but as the tasks of mourning are completed in different ways and at different speeds the person who has been bereaved is able to integrate the loss, to accept that parting has happened. The cord between life and death has been cut and we are able to say with thankfulness 'they were' rather than in grief saying 'they are no more'. For to live in the hearts of those we leave behind is not to die. The past is only a burden for those who forget it.

In the Iona Community we do not forget those of our number who have died. On the 31st day of the month we remember them.

We remember them with gratitude and love for all they gave us and meant to us.

They too have passed through the process, the preparation. But, however long they had to prepare (for some death was sudden and unexpected), the same feelings of shock and disbelief, anger and sadness, denial and fear, hope and acceptance can be present. It seems impertinent even to speak of it in the face of the courage of people like Brian and Fiona, the fortitude of Keith, the sharp gentleness of Roger, the kindliness of Ralph and Hamish – we can all make our own list of those we knew – but unless we face death ourselves, how can we bear to come near the grief of others?

On the 31st day of the month, the Iona Community remembers those of its numbers who have died.

Kate McIlhagga

Easter Week Saturday

Prayer

God of all creation –
who cannot be contained by our boundaries
or our definitions –
light from beyond galaxies,
sea without a farther shore;
you are present in every distinct place,
in every moment of history.
You are here and now.
Help us to understand
that those from whom we are separated in life
by distance, by sea and land;
those from whom we are separated
by difference, by prejudice,
by language, by lack of communication;
and that those from whom we are separated in death,
by its long silence, its aching absence –
are each of them in your presence;
that beyond our horizons,
beyond our boundaries,
beyond our understanding,
they are in your embrace.
Amen

Jan Sutch Pickard

Easter Sunday

Readings:

Psalm 30:10–12; John 20:1–18

A sermon

It took a long time for Mark to find a church he could dance in. During hymns, through songs of praise. During sermons, sometimes – rocking and turning and spinning in his wheelchair. It took him a long time but finally he found one. 'It disturbs the congregation,' they'd told him. 'Makes people uncomfortable in church.'

'People are afraid I guess,' he told me. 'Afraid of joy.'

When Mark first started learning he danced in tight circles. God told him how it meant that God's disabled people are afraid, timid. Not loose. Not free. But then slowly, gradually he wheeled and danced and the circles grew bigger. It's not for himself that he dances, Mark says. It's for God – to dance in front of God, to express his gratitude and thankfulness, and how he's chosen joy finally, and wants others to choose joy too. To dance.

'People just sit in the pews, and benches along the back. And when they stand up to sing finally they hardly sway or close their eyes. Like they're crippled and broken.' Dance and help free the disabled, God told Mark.

Easter Sunday

We're sitting together making decorations for his wheelchair – tissue paper streamers, yellow and gold – for the dance tonight. Mark tells me about how he spent six months in hospital with double pneumonia, and pressure sores from lying that cut to the bone. Just to move was painful. Getting turned like lying on knives. He cried whole days. Asked God, Why? Felt like Job. Like Job did. When can I get up again, he cried, like in some psalm and God said: When you learn finally, really learn. He wanted to die, just wanted to die. It was too much pain all the time – at one point with his circulation they were afraid gangrene could set in in his foot and they'd have to amputate. But God said: No, you can't die, I'm not finished with you. You have inner healing to do. Then you can get up. You have work to do but you still won't listen.

'Lying there,' said Mark, 'there's not much to do but think. Think and talk to God. There's no way to get away. You try to, watch the TV and that, but you can't really anyway.'

Mark told me how, lying propped and positioned between locked bed rails, he was forced to really work through his feelings from his past: His separation from a woman born with a disability also. Their broken relationship, his hurt. His drinking. Above and below all, his broken relationship

with God. His anger at God for who God had made him, put him through to suffer.

Then – after six months lying broken in sorrow, with ulcers and sores eating him – Mark resurrected healed and whole and God said dance. OK, so dance. Stop abusing yourself, stop punishing yourself and others. Stop sitting with words. Dance resurrection. Dance joy. The good news. Dance for all God's disabled people and for their liberation. Mark doesn't care what people think, he has to dance. It's his purpose, his mission. There's a service tonight, a celebration, and we're blowing up and tying on coloured balloons.

Lately he's been dancing figure eights, Mark says. In the crossing – big, free figures. Flowing, spinning, gliding. 'For a while I was trying to figure out why exactly. And didn't know, so then stopped thinking about it and just danced. Feeling the flowing freedom of it. But then it came to me: If you put a figure eight on its side, you know what it's the sign of? … Infinity. It's infinity. It's dancing infinity.'

I smile and we sit in silence. Finishing up, Mark says to me: 'I wish my mother was alive.' 'Gets lonely?' I say. 'Yeah, sometimes. And the doctors all told my mother, told mom when I was a child that I'd never walk. That I'd

always need a wheelchair …' Mark smiles. 'But they never said I'd never dance. Never said that … Maybe she can see me. Dancing. Dancing now. I like to think of her like that … There, finished, nice huh? Well, I guess that's it. Thanks for the help. So, you dancin' tonight too?'

We find it so difficult to dance in this life:

Carrying the burden of responsibilities
the pressures of every day
the memory of past partners
the weight of the world, it seems like, sometimes

Afraid of what people might think
afraid of people judging us
(of God judging us)
afraid of looking foolish out there on the floor

Afraid we won't get the rhythm right
afraid dancing is for the chosen few
Feeling so weighed down with guilt and sin
we can't move with grace

There have been some amazing, beautiful and brave people who have taught me to dance. Taught me steps I keep on forgetting and have to relearn:

There was Mark …

There was Andrew:

I met Andrew in a nursing home where I was volunteer visiting. Andrew was 93 years old but looked about 65 (dancing had kept him young). He lived in the home with his wife, Olive, who had some form of advanced dementia.

Andrew spent his days helping the nurses care for his wife – helping to clean and change and feed her. In his spare time he talked into the tape recorder by his bed; talked gently to Olive who didn't answer any more; talked to God in the little stained-glass chapel.

We would sit together out on the patio and he'd tell me his story: About fighting in the First World War as a 'Jack tar', leaving from Scapa Flow when he was fifteen and a half. About fighting in Gallipoli. About another time, out in the foggy, cold Atlantic, arriving too late to save friends blown to bits by a U-boat; fishing for arms and legs, feeling sick with grief and the horror of war.

About his merchant marine days and going on shore leave in Singapore. Strolling into a brothel there that he didn't realise was a brothel – he was only looking for a beer – and suddenly getting caught up in a brawl and getting thrown out of a window; falling three storeys into a cushioning heap of sewage and rubbish and then having to go back and report to his commanding officer. About driving a school bus for years. About getting gangrene somehow and losing his legs. About coming home from hospital.

We'd talk a while, and then he'd put some music on his phonograph and start dancing. Balanced, as graceful as any dancer, on his bed, his shorts rolled up, free leg stubs swinging gaily to and fro to a recording of Scottish Highland music. I'd watch him dancing and he was like light to me. Amazing – how someone can go through so much in their life and still dance: lose their wife, lose friends, lose their legs, and still dance.

'Any regrets?' I asked him, up over the spirited music.

'I saw the world,' he said, 'and had a warm, wee house … I'm thankful,' he sang.

There was Elizabeth:

I met Elizabeth working in a psychiatric hospital. (It was a place where few of the patients kept track of the days. Either they were unable to – lost in a fog of heavy drugs – or, because the days were all the same, they didn't bother.)

Elizabeth had an amazing and inexhaustible wardrobe and made a point of dressing up extravagantly. She sometimes changed as often as four times a day! And standing, smiling, in a long, flowing, golden gown, a floppy hat – both too big for the short old woman who looked like a little girl trying on her mother's outfits – long, white gloves, bright-red lipstick, costume pearls, dangling earrings in the shapes of moons and fishes – she explained proudly: 'I dress this way, darling, because the days are all the same. And if the dirty old days won't change then, by Jesus, I will!'

Through the long afternoons she danced. In the dirty, fold-up dining room. To a music only she could hear. All around her gathered the ghosts of the place – the suicides, the walking dead.

I danced with her sometimes when I was on duty and she taught me

new steps. Taught me how to open up and hear the music. Taught me how to dance no matter what.

There was the rainbow man:

I met the rainbow man working in a night shelter for homeless men. The rainbow man dressed in bright colours, too – tie-dyed t-shirts, purple hair, pink nail polish. Spoke in colours. It was a depressing, colourless place – dingy, dirty yellow walls. Clouds of grey smoke hanging. He was labelled mentally ill, schizophrenic. At one time he had studied fine arts at college, somebody said, had worked masterfully in oils and acrylics. Now, he worked in Crayola crayon. Drew like a child: dogs and cats and upside down pink-orange flowers planted in clouds. He got beat up by the men a lot.

One day he brought a leaf in from a walk he took (he was always taking long walks) and held it up to me and said *to look, see the light in the leaf pulsing, dancing still.*

I was busy and tired and had forgotten how to see, and said: 'Yeah, it's a maple leaf, so what.' I was oppressed and harried: there was someone buzzing at the door again, paperwork, so many important things to do. 'The light in the leaf,' he said again and danced away in a whirl of wind.

And when I sat down and stopped, I realised that

what he meant was: to look and see that energy, that essence, alive in the leaf. He could see it. He was supposed to be disabled but he was able to see the light of God in a leaf and to wonder at it. After weeks of running blind through my life the rainbow man taught me to open my eyes and heart again.

The most significant thing to me about these people, these friends, is that they are living the resurrection experience. They to me are the Christ. Christ in the stranger's guise: walking a road of trials, suffering, enduring crucifixion – maybe daily crucifixion. But, in the end, through their belief in life – through their partnership, connection, union with God – they are able to transform the darkness to light, suffering to joy, death to life.

> *O Lord …*
> *You have turned my mourning into*
> *dancing;*
> *you have taken off my sackcloth*
> *and clothed me with joy,*
> *so that my soul may praise you and*
> *not be silent*
> *O Lord my God, I will give thanks*
> *to you for ever.*

They are individuals with profound, deeply rooted faith. Faith in life. Faith in eternal life. Rubem Alves writes: 'Hope is hearing the melody of the future. Faith is to dance to it.'

Their lives are a witness. They are wounded healers. Prophets, teaching us how to dance, teaching us about the art of resurrection and how to open up to the music. The prophets aren't dead. They are sitting in nursing homes, in night shelters, in psychiatric hospitals, in dark pubs, in deep, lonely parks. They are sitting right beside you. Look.

It's difficult to dance. At times we feel entombed. Feel dead for days, months, years … But then it can happen. God's voice calls us out and we're alive again, in the light.

It could happen on a day when you're shrouded and wrapped in routine. And you suddenly stop for some reason, and see the graceful way light dances on the water, or shines in a path across paperwork – and it's beautiful, miraculous again. Life.

It could happen with a healing warm word that touches you, and your heart opens to embrace the light.

It could happen through prayer that suddenly, finally opens up, and you meet Jesus standing there: like a lover ready to take your hand.

It could happen walking down the road, and suddenly you look and see all the little flowers growing up between the cracks, blinding white in the summer light. And you bend down, feeling love again, blooming somehow; feeling the wonder of each precious petal (after days of walking around with your head down, feeling nothing); sun coming out (after days of feeling grey). And you look down the road and see all the little moments scattered along it. And the road says: life is full of little resurrections. And Jesus says: look at the birds of the air, they neither sow nor reap yet your heavenly father feeds them. And the sky says dive into life again.

(And sometimes it doesn't happen and we have to – instead of dance – keep falling until we hit bottom like the hollow of God's hand, and we are held there in Love to rest a while, before we start walking again. And maybe falling is a kind of dance anyway. A dance God finds just as beautiful as a wheelchair waltz. A gig, a reel, a tango …

And it can happen in the partnership of talking and listening. The communion of the moment. Sharing our stories and lives like the bread and wine.

Kathy Galloway writes: 'This is the meaning of the resurrection, that we can dance.'

Prayer

O Christ, Lord of the Dance
in you we live and move and
have our being

Through your body and blood
our sins are forgiven
and all we carry which is heavy
you take upon yourself

So that we may dance again

and give thanks
and celebrate life

Let us celebrate
Let us share the bread and the wine
the bread that dances with the atoms of the revolving earth
the wine that shimmers with the light of the Christ's Love
Amen

Neil Paynter

Easter Sunday

Easter blessing

How beautiful is the blossom
spilling from the tree,
the hidden primrose
and the bluebell
ringing out the news.
He is risen
he is alive
we shall live
for evermore.
The dark winter is past,
the slow, cold, foggy days are over.
May the warmth of your resurrection
touch our hearts and minds
as the warmth of the sun
blesses our bodies.

Kate McIlhagga

Easter Sunday

Easter brings liberation

When I was a small child, I used to think that the Easter story was a kind of 'spiritual story' in which a good God somehow overcame a 'bad' world. Or to put it another way, I thought Easter could in some rather vague way make me a better person than I was. Later in my life, when I had experienced the power of the Holy Spirit working in my own life, I realised that what had happened on that first Easter morning was that God in his love had transformed all powers of death and darkness into the powers of life and light – for all time, and for eternity. And that my own individual life was caught up in that cosmic movement of transformation. I knew that Easter had both a personal and a universal dimension. It was not just about 'me' – and my personal spiritual journey – it was also God's way of telling us that he was not a distant, remote God, but a God of love and power working in every situation of human experience. Binding up the broken-hearted, bringing good news to the oppressed and proclaiming a new kind of liberation – liberation from personal failure and liberation from all those man-made structures which today are robbing so many of our brothers and sisters of their human dignity and worth.

… We can never 'celebrate' Easter in isolation from the cries of our world. The moment we 'celebrate' Easter in some isolated way – in our little comfortable way – we make a mockery of Christ. We reduce the message of Easter – and in that process we domesticate Jesus so that he becomes some powerless household idol.

Easter Sunday

But when our hearts and minds are open to the wounds of our world today, we begin to see, in a hundred new ways, the meaning of the first Easter. Never just a 'spiritual' message, but something far more significant. A transforming and living God who has entered completely into the human condition.

> With the beckoning and dawning of another day,
> can the fragile, yet extraordinary
> words of Jesus
> propel us to a wider awareness,
> a gentler compassion?
> To the rediscovery of the sacred in ourselves,
> and in our world?
> To that risk-taking place
> where the imprisoning bonds
> of our self-enclosed lives are finally shattered?
> To a different journey
> in a listening companionship
> with the prophets of our time –
> the wounded and weary
> who announce the Kingdom
> and carry in their stories the seeds of the morrow?

Easter Sunday

The 'hidden ones'
in our global culture,
whose pain and joy
when threaded through our lives
enlarge the heart
and bring new meaning
to our common future:
that 'sacred future'
where, impossible as it may seem,
we 'love our neighbours as ourselves'.

Peter Millar

The Emmaus Road

Reading:
Luke 24:13–35

Steps
(Iona 1997)

When you live on an island
everything happens
somewhere else, they say.
These small dancing steps
on the sand
to the rhythm of sea
and music of wind
are a story waiting to begin
in another place.

Now, as far inland
as it is possible
to be, I can't pick out
the steps you taught us
then, or bring to mind

the name of the dance
the four of us did,
on the beach.
But I remember the pattern,
the weaving and threading
the shape and sharing
of a turning point.
I remember hands held out
and hands clasped;
I remember, against a greying sky,
dancing
into the sun again.

Joy Mead

Story from the road

When I left Iona after Easter week, I wondered if I'd ever meet Jesus again – in the 'real world'.

The week had been so powerful for me. The coming together of so many things in my time on Iona. In my life. Sitting in the cloisters and crying after the Maundy Thursday service – after Jesus was arrested, and the communion table was stripped and draped in black. The waiting in desolation and depression. And then, on Easter Sunday – Resurrection. Lighting candles at midnight and singing *Christ Be Our Light*. Hugging everyone.

So Iona, for me, was a place where I finally started to face the issues in my life. Issues like abandonment, betrayal, death … I started seeing patterns in my life, and in the life of the world. I began seeing how Jesus's story was, as they say, 'a story to live by'. Christ started to live in me. In my flesh and blood.

I was feeling down when I left the island, emotional – I hadn't felt that emotional in a long time. A real grief: leaving community and all we had shared living and working together. I felt wrung out, but hopeful. Vulnerable, but open.

I left with a group; we shared a meal on the ferry to Oban – bread and cheese and a thermos of tea – and did the morning office together. Then, gradually, we all went our separate ways: out into the world. All the witnesses – dispersed. We would keep in touch, we said. Write letters. I had some tough times, some dead ends it seemed like. But I tried to remain hopeful and disciplined. Then it started to happen: I visited a man I knew who was living in a nursing home. He was talking to me. About his life. He'd had a stroke. He was writing everything down so that he could remember, he said – the names of things and the people who came to visit him. Still, life was good: he enjoyed the music appreciation and poetry evenings they had at the home, the good food. The view out back of the pine and cedar trees – evergreen scent with the windows wide and curtains dancing.

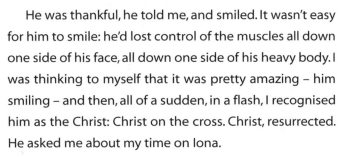

He was thankful, he told me, and smiled. It wasn't easy for him to smile: he'd lost control of the muscles all down one side of his face, all down one side of his heavy body. I was thinking to myself that it was pretty amazing – him smiling – and then, all of a sudden, in a flash, I recognised him as the Christ: Christ on the cross. Christ, resurrected. He asked me about my time on Iona.

Talking to him, sitting with him there, healed me in a way.

I visited my folks. We had grown closer somehow. My mother told me things I never knew about her – things she had gone through growing up. She was telling me a story, and suddenly the lines in her face in the soft, late-evening light were beautiful: there was an agony in the garden traced there; but a sign of the resurrection somehow, too.

Then I met a homeless man in London, in Euston station. We were talking intensely: about life, about suffering. But about how wonderful and mysterious and incredible life is, too. We shared his bottle and my fish and chips between us. He had a very profound under-standing – well, he'd been through a lot in his life. A lot of abandonment, betrayal, death … Every day I guess: waking up in the park, walking down the road into the city to be crucified by the state, by the crowds, by his self.

Easter Sunday

We were very honest with each other. He shared a poem he'd written; recited it by heart with his eyes closed. I started to cry, it was so beautiful. I can't say what it was about, exactly. It was the way he spoke and sang it. Something in his broken, scarred voice. In his transfigured, life-lined face. It was like the poem was light and resurrection above all the pain and suffering – all the pain and suffering in the world. I turned to thank him but he had gone, disappeared. I saw him later, walking ahead of me; shuffling and stumbling through the crowd at King's Cross station.

Sometimes I recognise Christ in moments like that. Other times, it's more in the everyday: sharing good news or lunch with a friend; turning and meeting a stranger's smile; in company of a partner as we journey along, or pause somewhere in the heart of silence – moments like that. I try to remain open to it. It's not always easy.

'Greetings,' I wrote to my Iona friend. 'Christ is risen! So, have you seen him?'

He responded, on a postcard of a city sunrise: 'Christ is risen! He is risen indeed! Yes.'

He's doing volunteer work. I'm getting ideas of going back to school – nursing maybe, community work? Terry is working midnights at a corner shop in Sheffield: it's not the job, he says, it's the people. The people who come in off the cold, mean streets; talking to them at all hours. Listening – if he can just learn to stay open, he says.

Julie is travelling. Last time Ray heard she was somewhere in South India. It's all a road, it's all a pilgrimage – life – wherever you are. I still feel we're all connected. Who knows, maybe we'll meet again one day.

I have moments sometimes when I can see light radiating and glancing off everything, everyone. It's like the light I witnessed on Iona: that beautiful, warm, amazing light falling, like God's glowing grace, on the Ross of Mull; shining on the sea.

They say that Iona is 'a thin place': a place where the separation between the material and the spiritual realm is only tissue-thin. It's tissue-thin everywhere I'm discovering: in India; in Euston Station; in hometowns; in lonely, desperate corner shops at drunken midnight …

Everywhere, I want to cry, and shout, 'Hallelujah – yes!'

Neil Paynter

Prayer

Christ, you are before us.
This is what gives us courage to go on.
It is you who directs.
It is you who beckons.
So we dedicate ourselves.
And we bless you now.

George MacLeod

125

Easter Sunday

Affirmation

We believe in a bright and amazing God
who has been to the depths of despair
on our behalf;
who has risen in splendour and majesty;
who decorates the universe
with sparkling water, clear white light,
twinkling stars and sharp colours,
over and over and over again.

We believe that Jesus is the light of the world;
that God believes in us, and trusts us,
even though we make the same mistakes
over and over and over again.

We commit ourselves
to Jesus,
to one another as brothers and sisters,
and to the Maker's business in the world.

God said: Let there be light.
Amen

Helen Lambie

Beyond Easter

Reach out your hands, Thomas

Reading: John 20:19–31

After thirty years of living and working ecumenically, I am convinced that in every circumstance where the Holy Spirit leads us, if we choose to follow, is to the place of gospel, of good news. This is the place where the marks are visible, where people hear their names called with love, where people break open their lives to share them, where people bear witness. This is where Jesus finds us, knows us, loves us, heals us, sets us free and calls us to follow him. Furthermore, I am convinced that the place of the gospel is rarely inside a church. The place of the gospel is the world.

The place of the gospel is the world, where women gather at the well, meet the living Christ, are included, respected and called to a ministry of proclamation. So I have encountered a dynamic and committed ecumenical faith, and its expression in worship, among women working together across denominations in a way that leaves many of their male counterparts standing, defending an authority that seems to derive more from power to control than from the powerlessness of the cross.

The place of the gospel is the world, where Dives continues to ignore the beseechings of Lazarus. So I have encountered a dynamic and committed ecumenical faith, and its expression in worship, among poor people and the people who share their lives and their struggle for justice.

The place of the gospel is the world, where a prodigal son shows what it means to be generous in human relationships. So I have encountered a dynamic and committed ecumenical faith, and its expression in worship, among counsellors and carers and people with AIDS and community activists who seek to heal what is broken, reunite what is separated and re-create the face of the earth.

I could go on – about people working in peacemaking, industrial relations, the health service, race relations, among young people. I could go on about local ecumenical projects and communities, the considerable numbers of people crossing denominations to study everything from the Bible to pastoral care and contemplative spirituality … but you know what I am saying. The place of the gospel is never abstract or academic, nor is it theoretical and dogmatic. It is always the place of engagement with the world. It is the place where the Word becomes flesh, where you can see the marks in the side …

Kathy Galloway

Thomas

Put your hand,
Thomas,
on the crawling head
of a child
imprisoned
in a cot
in Romania.

Place your finger,
Thomas,
on the list of those
who have disappeared
in Chile.

Stroke the cheek,
Thomas,
of the little girl
sold in prostitution
in Thailand.

Touch, Thomas,
the gaping wounds
of my world.

Feel, Thomas,
the primal wound
of my people.

Reach out your hands,
Thomas,
and place them at the side of the poor.

Grasp my hands, Thomas,
and believe.

Kate McIlhagga

129

Beyond Easter

Stooge Jesus

He was our April Fool
hanging on a tree in spring,
a king to mock and sniff at

He was the world's buffoon,
throwing his arms around lepers
like there was no tomorrow

He was a clown
in the circus of the temple
Except no one laughed
at his table-throwing turn that day

Stooge Jesus
taking the knocks from us
The divine comedian.

He was a straight man
to the puffed-up priests
who used his new commandments
as their feed lines

If he'd been a woman
he'd have been their Aunt Sally
set up for a knock down:

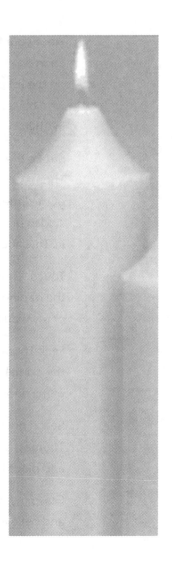

An apology for a messiah
he seemed to those
who wanted a warrior not a peace-full fool

An eccentric, he was
to those whose lives he changed in public
then told to keep it secret

What a queer fish
filling Peter's nets with:
feeding the five thousand with:
eating resurrection breakfast with:
queer fish

What a caution
to the daughters of Jerusalem

The Son of God's a kidder

Stooge Jesus
Taking custard pies in his face for ever
The divine comedian.

John Davies

Beyond Easter

The cross of victory

Reading: Colossians 2:8–15

When the first Christians began to meet in secret in the catacombs of Rome, we know that they used to mark their meeting places with secret signs. One was the fish – whose initial letters, in Greek, stood for 'Jesus Christ, Son of God, Saviour'. Another, to begin with, was the cross.

But with the cross, apparently, there was a problem – at least, for some. For to some the cross still stood for shame and defeat – whereas they knew themselves to be participants not in defeat, but in victory.

So they searched around for a sign that would turn the cross of shame into the cross of victory. And they found it in the circlet of laurel leaves that was used to crown the victor's head in the Roman games – the Gold Medal of ancient times. And so, with the circle round the centre, the cross of defeat was clearly seen for what it really was – a cross of victory indeed.

Our God has won, in Christ, a victory so vast that it surely deserves the clearest victory sign that we can find …

So, what sort of sign can we raise, to celebrate the vastness of the victory that God has won in Christ? In Colossians, Paul writes:

'On the cross Christ freed himself from the power of the spiritual rulers and authorities; he made a public spectacle of them by leading them as captives in his victory procession.'

Are we not the people who have been set free, by Christ, from these powers? Narrow nationalism, blind ideology, superstitious and lazy religion, servitude to violence within and war without, the deadly divisions of race and class and ideology – have we not been liberated, by Christ, from all of these? For us, in George MacLeod's famous phrase, the under-taker has come and gone – we are dead to our sins, and our ransomed lives are now hidden with Christ in God. Now, is it not required of us that we live out, in hard yet joyful discipline, the nature of the new life in the midst of the suffering of the world, with God's help?

For it is we, incredibly, who are to be the victory sign. When people look at us, at our ransomed and renewed lives, they are to see, with God's help, not us but the life of the risen Christ – and turn and follow him.

John Harvey

Beyond Easter

A prayer for our own reshaping

O Christ, the Master carpenter,
who at the last, through wood and nails,
purchased our whole salvation,
wield well your tools in the workshop of your world,
so that we who come rough-hewn to your bench
may here be fashioned to a truer beauty of your hand.
We ask it for your own name's sake.
Amen

George MacLeod

Blessing

May the joy, and the confidence, of Easter be ours,
both in our personal lives,
and in our life of obedience and discipleship in the world.

John Harvey

The Ascension

No other plans

There is a very old legend, and all legends that persist speak truth, concerning the return of the Lord Jesus Christ to heaven after his Ascension. It is said that the angel Gabriel met him at the gates of the city.

'Lord, this is a great salvation that thou hast wrought,' said the angel. But the Lord Jesus only said, 'Yes.'

'What plans hast thou made for carrying on the work? How are all to know what thou hast done?' asked Gabriel.

'I left Peter and James and John and Martha and Mary to tell their friends, their friends to tell their friends, till all the world should know.'

'But Lord Jesus,' said Gabriel, 'suppose Peter is too busy with the nets, or Martha with the housework, or the friends they tell are too occupied, and forget to tell their friends – what then?'

The Lord Jesus did not answer at once; then he said in his quiet wonderful voice: 'I have not made any other plans. I am counting on them.'

George MacLeod

Loving kindness and God's grace

Reading: Micah 6:8

Cheerfulness – loving kindness, as Micah puts it – is about how we relate to others, about hospitality, warmth, openness, about our responsibility towards one another, about neighbourly concern, and belonging together in the bundle of life. Cheerfulness is not about the kind of frothy joy that denies the pain or seriousness of life's travails. On the contrary, cheerfulness confronts adversity in full recognition of its reality, but it looks through the darkness. Cheerfulness is the persistent tortoise that keeps on keeping on and gets there in the end; cheerfulness is the resilient toy that you cannot knock over; cheerfulness survives every setback and disappointment because it reflects the resurrection-hope and the faith that God's grace is sufficient for all our needs.

Norman Shanks

Prayer for the Iona Community

O God, who gave to your servant Columba
the gifts of courage, faith and cheerfulness,
and sent people forth from Iona
to carry the word of your gospel to every creature:
grant, we pray, a like spirit to your church,
even at this present time.
Further in all things the purpose of our community,
that hidden things be revealed to us,
and new ways to touch the hearts of all.
May we preserve with each other
sincere charity and peace,
and, if it be your holy will,
grant that this place of your abiding be continued still
to be a sanctuary and a light.
through Jesus Christ.
Amen

George MacLeod

Reading: John 10:10–11

Sources

Page 15 'Invocation for Lent' by Kate McIlhagga, from *The Pattern of Our Days: Liturgies and Resources for Worship*, edited by Kathy Galloway (Wild Goose Publications, 1996).

Page 17 Extract by Ron Ferguson is from his book *Chasing the Wild Goose: The Story of the Iona Community* (Wild Goose Publications, 1998).

Pages 18 & 22 Opening and closing responses by Brian Woodcock, from an Ash Wednesday Service, Michael Chapel, Iona.

Page 23 'Ashes' by Kathy Galloway, previously appeared in *Coracle* (the journal of the Iona Community), Issue 3/38.

Page 33 'Greenpeace estimates …', quote by Helen Steven from the article 'Assault on the Poor', *Coracle*, Issue 3/12.

Page 33 'Cosmic Golgotha' by George MacLeod from *Daily Readings with George MacLeod*, edited by Ron Ferguson (Wild Goose Publications, 2001). Originally appeared in *Coracle*, 1965.

Page 35 'The Way to Peace' by Kate McIlhagga from *Maker's Blessing* (Wild Goose Publications, 2000). Originally appeared as 'Prayer Rosary' in *The Pattern of our Days* (see above).

Page 36 Affirmation by Brian Woodcock and Jan Sutch Pickard from *The Iona Abbey Worship Book* (Wild Goose Publications, 2001).

Page 47 Extract by Runa Mackay is from *Exile in Israel: A Personal Journey with the Palestinians* (Wild Goose Publications, 1995).

Page 59 Extract from 'Weeping for cities and working for justice' by Ruth Burgess from *Praying for the Dawn: A Resource Book for the Ministry of Healing*, by Ruth Burgess & Kathy Galloway (Wild Goose Publications, 2000).

Page 63 Extract by George MacLeod is from 'A Chaos of Uncalculating Love', in *The Whole Earth Shall Cry Glory: Iona Prayers* (Wild Goose Publications, 1985).

Page 63 'Ducks, hens and a black goat' by Peter Millar is from the chapter 'Celebrating' contained in *Waymarks: Signposts to Discovering God's Presence in the World* (Canterbury Press, Peter W. Millar, 2000, ISBN 1-85311-336-0).

Page 66 'Peacemakers in a changing world' is an extract from the article 'Being a Peacemaker in a Changing World' by Helen Steven, *Coracle*, Issue 3/7.

Page 81 'Gethsemane Prayer' by Jan Sutch Pickard first appeared in *Vice Versa* (Church in the Market Place Publications, Buxton Methodist Church, Buxton, Derbyshire SK17 6HS, 1997, ISBN 1 889147 12 8).

Page 82 'Once more' by Kate McIlhagga from *Praying for the Dawn: A Resource Book for the Ministry of Healing*, by Ruth Burgess & Kathy Galloway (Wild Goose Publications, 2000).

Page 83 Extracts from the articles 'Envy of Prisoners' and 'Glory in the Grey', which appeared in *Coracle*, Issues 3/27 and 3/7.

Page 84 'Prison Quartet' by Jan Sutch Pickard first appeared in *Vice Versa* (Church in the Market Place Publications, Buxton Methodist Church, Buxton, Derbyshire SK17 6HS, 1997, ISBN 1 889147 12 8).

Page 91 'Simon carries the cross': the story of Sam also appears in *A Need for Living: Signposts on the Journey of Life and Beyond* by Tom Gordon (Wild Goose Publications, 2001).

Page 94 Extract by George MacLeod originally appeared in *Only One Way Left* and is quoted in *Chasing the Wild Goose: The Story of the Iona Community*, by Ron Ferguson (Wild Goose Publications, 1998).

Page 95 'Prayer of the crucified' by Jan Sutch Pickard originally appeared in *Imaginary Conversations: Dialogues for Use in Worship and Bible Study* (Methodist Church Overseas Division, 1989/90).

Page 101 'The work of grief' by Kate McIlhagga is taken from 'About the work of grief' which first appeared in *Coracle*, Issue 3/10.

Page 104 Prayer by Jan Sutch Pickard is taken from the 'Service for All Souls' which appears in *Praying for the Dawn* (see opposite).

Page 105 Easter Sunday reading by Neil Paynter is based on 'Wounded Healers' from *Praying for the Dawn* (see opposite). The quotation from Rubem A. Alves is from *The Poet, the Warrior, the Prophet: The Edward Cadbury Lectures 1990* (published by SCM, now out of print.)

Page 114 'This is the meaning of the resurrection' quote by Kathy Galloway is from *A Prayer to the Trinity: Celebrating Women* (new edition) edited by Hannah Ward, Jennifer Wild & Janet Morley (SPCK, 1995, ISBN 0-281-04836-3).

Page 116 'Easter Blessing' by Kate McIlhagga is from *Praying for the Dawn* (see above).

Sources

Page 117 'Easter brings liberation' by Peter Millar is an extract from *Letters from Madras*, Dorothy and Peter Millar, 1988.

Page 118 'With the beckoning and dawning' by Peter Millar is from *Seeds for the Morrow, Inspiring Thoughts from Many Sources*, collected by Dorothy Millar.

Page 125 'Christ you are before us' by George MacLeod appears in *The Iona Abbey Worship Book* (Wild Goose Publications, 2001).

Page 126 Affirmation by Helen Lambie is from *The Iona Abbey Worship Book* (see above).

Page 127 'Reach out your hands, Thomas' by Kathy Galloway is an extract from the essay 'Put Your hand in My Side' which appeared in *For God's Sake ... Unity: An Ecumenical Voyage with the Iona Community*, edited by Maxwell Craig (Wild Goose Publications, 1998).

Page 128 'Thomas' by Kate McIlhagga first appeared in *The Pattern of Our Days: Liturgies and Resources for Worship*, edited by Kathy Galloway (Wild Goose Publications, 1996).

Page 132 'The cross of victory' by John Harvey is taken from 'Suffering and Victory – Two Reflections', *Coracle*, Issue 3/7.

Page 134 'A prayer for our own reshaping' by George MacLeod appears in *The Iona Abbey Worship Book* (see above).

Page 134 Blessing by John Harvey first appeared in his Leader's Letter, *Coracle*, Issue 3/21.

Page 135 'No other plans' by George MacLeod is from *Daily Readings with*

George MacLeod, edited by Ron Ferguson (Wild Goose Publications, 2001).

Page 137 'Loving kindness and God's Grace' by Norman Shanks is an extract from the sermon 'Engagement, not Escape', Iona Abbey, 8 June 1997, which appeared in *Coracle*, August 1997.

Page 138 'Prayer for the Iona Community' by George MacLeod appears in *The Iona Abbey Worship Book* (see opposite).

Contributors

Helen Boothroyd's professional training is in town planning and she also has many years' voluntary experience of justice and peace work. An associate of the Iona Community, she was part of the resident staff at the Abbey on Iona for three years. She is currently setting up a new retreat centre with her husband (see entry under *Richard Moriarty* for more information).

Anna Briggs was born on Tyneside in 1947, eldest of six girls, brought up in Christianity and socialism and adding feminism to the mix. She is a writer, actor, artist, hymnwriter, survivor, clown – endlessly fascinated with people, what makes us all tick, what makes us feel valued and part of community, what is our true self.

Ruth Burgess lives in Sunderland and is a community development worker on North Tyneside. A writer of liturgies, prayers and poetry, she recently edited *A Book of Blessings* (Wild Goose Publications, 2001). She enjoys fireworks and growing flowers and vegetables, and is a member of the Iona Community.

Joyce Gunn Cairns works as an artist; her work is included in the permanent collection of the Scottish National Portrait Gallery in Edinburgh. About her vocation she writes: 'I have as much passion as Frank Auerbach but unlike him I do not live and work in my studio from dawn to dusk, 364 days a year. Would I leave brothers and sisters* if I could paint with Auerbach's intensity, or is it because I don't that I can't?' (*Mt 19:29)

Maxwell Craig and his wife Janet live in Dunblane; they have four children and two grandchildren. They spent fifteen months from 1999 to 2000 at St

Contributors

Andrew's Scots Kirk in Jerusalem. Maxwell is a minister of the Church of Scotland and has served parishes in Falkirk, Glasgow and Aberdeen; he was General Secretary of ACTS (Action of Churches Together in Scotland) from 1990 to 1998 and is a member of the Iona Community.

Erik Cramb is a son of post-war working class Glasgow. He worked in the Butcher's youth club in the east end of Glasgow whilst a theological student at Trinity College. After parish ministries in St Thomas's Gallowgate in Glasgow, St Paul's Kirk in Kingston, Jamaica, and back to Yoker in Glasgow, he became a full-time Industrial Chaplain in Dundee in 1989. Currently the National Organiser of Scottish Churches Industrial Mission, he is the author of *Parables and Patter* (Wild Goose Publications, now out of print).

John Davies is a member of the Iona Community living and working in Liverpool, where he is an Anglican parish priest. He is a freelance writer and poet, and wrote 'Stooge Jesus' for the Greenbelt Christian arts festival, which he has been involved in for 23 years.

Ron Ferguson is a former Leader of the Iona Community. The author of several books, including a biography of George MacLeod, founder of the Iona Community, he is now a full-time writer and broadcaster.

Kathy Galloway is a member of the Iona Community. She is a theologian and writer and Linkworker for Scotland for Church Action on Poverty. She lives in Glasgow.

Tom Gordon has been chaplain at the Edinburgh Marie Curie Centre for eight years, having previously worked as a Church of Scotland minister in two Edinburgh parishes. He writes and teaches on spiritual and pastoral care and is author of *A Need for Living* (Wild Goose Publications, 2001). He is married to Mary, and both are members of the Iona Community. They have three grown-up children.

John Harvey is a member of the Iona Community, currently working as an Interim Minister with the Church of Scotland. He served as Warden of Iona Abbey from 1971 to 1976, and as Leader of the Community from 1988 to 1995. He is married to Molly, also a member, and they live in Glasgow.

Ruth Harvey is editor of *Coracle*, the journal of the Iona Community. She is a member of the Iona Community and lives in Cumbria.

Helen Lambie is a baker and caterer from Biggar, Lanarkshire; she recently spent three years on Iona as part of the Community's resident group there.

Kate McIlhagga is a retired United Reformed Church minister living in Northumberland and is a writer, retreat giver and grandmother. She works as a volunteer at the local hospice and is a member of the Iona Community and of its area of concern which explores spirituality.

Runa Mackay graduated in medicine in 1944 and specialised in paediatrics. In 1955 she went out to do a locum for six months in the Edinburgh Medical Missionary Hospital (EMMS) in Nazareth, Israel, and has worked in the Middle East ever since, in Israel, the Occupied Territories and Lebanon.

George MacLeod, the founder of the Iona Community, was a charismatic man of prayer and action whose life spanned the 20th century. Giving up a promising career as minister to the middle classes in Edinburgh, he took up a post in the poor and depressed area of Govan in Glasgow, where he moved inexorably towards socialism and pacifism and his theology became more mystical, cosmic and political. In 1938 he initiated the venture of restoring the ancient abbey on Iona, out of which the Iona Community developed.

Joy Mead is a new member of the Iona Community and a new grandma. She works freelance as poet, writer and editor and leads small creative writing groups. For many years she has been involved with justice and peace and development education groups. Poetry is her main interest and her poems have been included in many magazines and anthologies. She is author of *The One Loaf* (Wild Goose Publications, 2001).

Peter Millar, writer and activist, is a former Warden of Iona Abbey. For many years he and his late wife Dorothy worked in the Church of South India, and his books continue to reflect upon an engaged Christianity within an inter-connected world.

Richard Moriarty is a qualified teacher and craftsman, with a training in theology and scripture study. A member of the Iona Community, he met and married Helen Boothroyd (qv) while they were both working for three years on the resident staff at Iona Abbey. After leaving Iona, Richard and Helen ran a small house of welcome and retreat in South Cumbria. They are currently setting up a new retreat centre near Carlisle, offering guests the possibility of using creative media of art and crafts to explore spirituality and prayer. For more information write to: Stillicidia, Chapel View, Milton, Brampton, Cumbria, CA8 1JD. Tel: 016977 46821. E-mail: bookings@stillicidia.com

Neil Paynter worked as a resident and a volunteer with the Iona Community on Iona. Previously, he worked in the social work field.

Jan Sutch Pickard is currently Warden of the Abbey on Iona. A member of the Iona Community, she formerly worked as an editor of Methodist publications – a desk job – whereas she now enjoys leading pilgrimages over the hills. She is, to the best of her ability, she says, a preacher, a poet and a storyteller; a bread-maker and a picker-up of crumbs. She is the editor of *Dandelions and Thistles* and co-author of *Advent readings from Iona* (both Wild Goose Publications, 1999 & 2000)

Norman Shanks has been Leader of the Iona Community since 1995. Before training for ministry in the Church of Scotland he was a civil servant in the Scottish Office. He was convener of the Church of Scotland's Church and Nation Committee from 1988–92, and is currently a member of the Central Committee of the World Council of Churches and of the Board of Christian Aid.

David J.M. Coleman and Zam Walker Coleman met on Iona in 1995. David is a URC minister with a developing ecumenical project in Barrhead, and with interests in creative worship. Zam is active in women's spirituality issues. Both are members of the Iona Community. Their son Taliesin was born in 1999. Their second child is due to arrive imminently.

Brian Woodcock is a member of the Iona Community, and a United Reformed Church minister in St Albans and Bricket Wood. He was Warden of Iona Abbey from 1998 to 2001, and is an associate of the church and community develop-ment training agency, Avec. He is co-author of *Advent Readings from Iona*.

The Iona Community

The Iona Community, founded in 1938 by the Revd George MacLeod, then a parish minister in Glasgow, is an ecumenical Christian community committed to seeking new ways of living the Gospel in today's world. Initially working to restore part of the medieval abbey on Iona, the Community today remains committed to 'rebuilding the common life' through working for social and political change, striving for the renewal of the church with an ecumenical emphasis, and exploring new, more inclusive approaches to worship, all based on an integrated understanding of spirituality.

The Community now has over 240 Members, about 1500 Associate Members and around 1500 Friends. The Members – women and men from many denominations and backgrounds (lay and ordained), living throughout Britain with a few overseas – are committed to a fivefold Rule of devotional discipline, sharing and accounting for use of time and money, regular meeting, and action for justice and peace.

At the Community's three residential centres – the Abbey and the MacLeod Centre on Iona, and Camas Adventure Camp on the Ross of Mull – guests are welcomed from March to October and over Christmas. Hospitality is provided for over 110 people, along with a unique opportunity, usually through week-long programmes, to extend horizons and forge relationships through sharing an experience of the common life in worship, work, discussion and relaxation. The Community's shop on Iona, just outside the Abbey grounds, carries an attractive range of books and craft goods.

The Community's administrative headquarters are in Glasgow, which also serves as a base for its work with young people, the Wild Goose Resource Group working in the field of worship, a bi-monthly magazine, *Coracle*, and a publishing house, Wild Goose Publications.

For information on the Iona Community contact:
The Iona Community
Fourth Floor, Savoy House,
140 Sauchiehall Street, Glasgow G2 3DH, UK
Phone: 0141 332 6343 Fax 0141 332 1090
e-mail: ionacomm@gla.iona.org.uk   web: www.iona.org.uk

For enquiries about visiting Iona, please contact:
Iona Abbey
Isle of Iona
Argyll PA76 6SN, UK
Phone: 01681 700404   e-mail: ionacomm@iona.org.uk

For book/tape/CD catalogues, contact:
Wild Goose Publications
Fourth Floor, Savoy House,
140 Sauchiehall Street, Glasgow G2 3DH, UK
Phone: 0141 332 6292 Fax 0141 332 1090
e-mail: admin@onabooks.com
or see our products online at www.ionabooks.com

More from Wild Goose Publications:

FOR LENT AND EASTER

Stages on the Way

Worship resources for Lent, Holy Week and Easter

Wild Goose Worship Group

This 'book of bits' for Lent and Easter worship, tracing Jesus's road to the cross, has the prime purpose of resourcing worship that enables people to sense the hope, apprehension and joy of Easter as felt by Jesus's friends. It offers a unique range and diversity of elements for lay and clergy worship enablers.

240pp · 1 901557 11 1 · £14.99

The Courage to Say No

Twenty-three songs for Lent and Easter from the Wild Goose Worship Group

John L. Bell & Graham Maule

Tracing the sometimes sure, sometimes faltering steps of Jesus and his followers through the entire season of Lent to Easter Day and then beyond, these songs allow us to reflect on their progress, enter their experience and ultimately make their confusion, doubt, joy and liberation our own. Many are in four-part harmony, which will be satisfying for choirs to sing, as well as being accessible to congregations.

Songbook: 96pp · 0 947988 78 5 · £7.99
Cassette (16 tracks): 0 947988 79 3 · £8.99

FOR LENT AND EASTER contd.

Enemy of Apathy

Sixty-two songs for Lent, Eastertide and Pentecost

John L. Bell & Graham Maule

Includes: Travelling the road to freedom ● Be still and know ● Jesus Christ is waiting ● Lord of the morning ● Kyrie/Sanctus & Benedictus/Agnus Dei (Kentigern setting)

Songbook: 144pp · 0 947988 27 0 · £8.99

FOR ADVENT

Advent Readings from Iona

Brian Woodcock & Jan Sutch Pickard

Celebrate Christmas with reflections and prayers for each day of Advent. This effective antidote to the commercialism of the festive season can be used for individual meditation or group worship.

96pp · 1 901557 33 2 · £7.99

Cloth for the Cradle

Worship resources and readings for Advent, Christmas and Epiphany

Wild Goose Worship Group

This rediscovery of the stories of Christ's birth through adult eyes contains much to reflect on individually and to use in group and worship situations. The Wild Goose Worship Group's innovative style of worship is widely admired and imitated

152pp · 1 901557 01 4 · £8.99

Also from Wild Goose Publications:

The Iona Abbey Worship Book

The Iona Community

Services and resources used daily in the Abbey on the island of Iona reflecting the Iona Community's commitment to the belief that worship is all that we are and all that we do, with no division into the 'sacred' and the 'secular'. The material draws on many traditions, including the Celtic.

272pp · 1 901557 50 2 · £9.99

A Book of Blessings

... and how to write your own

Ruth Burgess

A collection of blessings for the people, sadnesses, artefacts, special occasions and journeys of our lives. It also explores the tradition of blessings, including biblical and Celtic, and offers ideas and resources to encourage readers to write blessings of their own, with suggestions for how to organise a blessings workshop.

176pp · 1 901557 48 0 · £8.99

Daily Readings with George MacLeod

Ron Ferguson (ed)

Many lives were changed by George MacLeod's spine-tingling sermons, and many more by his example. The extracts in this book give a flavour of the passion and poetry of the Celtic mystic who led the rebuilding of Iona Abbey, and whose theology was worked out not in the study but out on the street.

126pp · 1 901557 55 3 · £8.99